JONATHAN EDWARDS, BEAUTY, AND YOUNGER EVANGELICALS

Jonathan Edwards, Beauty, and Younger Evangelicals

Adam Newcomb Boyd

JESociety Press

WWW.JESOCIETY.ORG

Paperback Edition September 16, 2019
ISBN 9780578579993
© 2019 Adam Newcomb Boyd

A publication of JESociety Press
Visit https://www.jesociety.org

All rights reserved. No part of this publication may be reproduced, distributed, or transmitted in any form or by any means, including photocopying, recording, or other electronic or mechanical methods, without the prior written permission of the author/publisher, except in the case of brief quotations embodied in critical reviews and certain other noncommercial uses permitted by copyright law.

For permission requests and inquiries,
Email: info@jesociety.org
Web: www.jesociety.org

Scripture quotations are taken from the English Standard Version ® ESV ®. Copyright © 2001 by Crossway Bibles.

PRAISE FOR THIS VOLUME

Edwards, Beauty and Younger Evangelicals is a book about what matters most. For those courageous enough to think deeply about what it means to have a relationship with the living God, Boyd's book is a joy. A unique study of Edwards' great work, *Religious Affections,* the book challenges readers to consider Edwards' timeless insights on knowing and experiencing the beauty of Christ as revealed in the Scriptures. Through keen awareness of the cultural world inhabited by both Edwards and younger evangelicals, the book offers a compelling case for appropriating Edwards' insights for the contemporary church. Moving beyond concepts, the reader is provided a hands-on tool for building the bridge from the past to the present.

S. Donald Fortson, III DMin, PhD
Professor of Church History and Practical Theology,
Director, DMin Program, Reformed Theological Seminary Charlotte

If you have a heart for today's youth to develop a mature Christian faith, this book is for you! Adam Boyd has given his life to minister to young people, and he has identified a vital narrative of today's youth: the need for authenticity. It means an authentic faith that connects biblical belief with the experience of Christ's beauty and the heartfelt affections for the matters of the Gospel. Using the brilliant work and thinking of Jonathan Edwards, one of the most influential Christian thinkers of the past three centuries, Adam offers both a solid foundation for how to address this contemporary yearning, and a practical and detailed action plan.

J. Maurer, PhD
President of Montreat College

Few things are as exciting as reading theology. It is a subject that gets at all the juiciest questions about life. And few theologians are as exciting to read as the American Puritan Jonathan Edwards (1703–58). If I were to guess, what you have heard about Edwards is probably at best a caricature and at worst simply untrue. For, Edwards is an uncommon thinker whose answers to questions in theology can be as juicy as the questions themselves. To be sure, a lot of what he wrote is hard to understand. But don't let that stop you. A welcome contribution to the ever-growing library of work on Edwards, Boyd takes up the critical subject of Edwards and Beauty and makes it understandable. Targeting the religious affections of teenagers, Boyd hits the bull's eye with *Jonathan Edwards, Beauty, and Younger Evangelicals*.

Mark Hamilton, PhD
Author of *A Treatise on Jonathan Edwards, Continuous Creation, and Christology* and *New England Dogmatics: A Systematic Collection of Questions and Answers in Divinity by Maltby Gelston (1766–1865)*

If you are a Jonathan Edwards' scholar—*what a time to be alive!* The Puritan pastor-theologian from the eighteenth century continues to prove to be one of the most compelling thinkers in all of Colonial American history, even the Western world for that matter. Like Da Vinci and other verifiable geniuses, Edwards contributed to Western thought as a true polymath. That is to say, just as Da Vinci was artist, architect, and inventor, so also Edwards was a pastor, theologian, missionary, and philosopher. In this book, Adam Newcomb Boyd provides another compelling deep dive into the thought life of Edwards. Beginning exegetically, Boyd surveys the Bible's general teaching on the affections, the deep longings and repulsions of the soul. After that, he considers one of Edwards' theological masterpieces, *Religious Affections*. Next, he places Edwards in his historical and philosophical context, comparing and contrasting him to Locke and Newton among others. Finally in the concluding sections, Boyd makes pastoral and ministerial application from all that has preceded. I continue to be grateful for the publishing ventures of JESociety, and for Boyd's newest contribution to our burgeoning field.

Matthew Everhard, DMin
Senior Pastor, Gospel Fellowship Presbyterian Church
Author of *A Theology of Joy: Jonathan Edwards and Eternal Happiness in the Holy Trinity*

To Ann,

whose encouragement, prayer and patience

made this project possible

and to our children

Mary Page, Joe and Hank—the church needs you!

Acknowledgements

This project has been a slow work, framed by hundreds of informal conversations, and several important, more structured contributions. This book grew out of my doctoral dissertation and with that in mind I am grateful to my academic advisor, Steve Childers, for his encouragement, guidance, and patience, as well as the seminary's support staff, Joyce Sisler and Lori Ginn. I am thankful to my faculty reader, Bob Orner, as well as Don Fortson for squaring my shoulders and pointing me to the most important material on Edwards.

Without the prayerful support of the staff at camps Merri-Mac and Timberlake, where I have served throughout these studies, this project would not have been possible. Particular thanks go to Dan Singletary for pointing to the gospel, Ryan Carlson for pointing to culture, John Menendez for pointing to community, and to my brother, Bobby Boyd for pointing to affective, Christ-centered devotion. Thanks also to our counselors, for listening, pushing back, demonstrating and leading toward "that which is life indeed." Your lives demonstrate Edwards's vision.

Additionally, I am grateful to Trinity Presbyterian Church, Asheville, and Christ Community Church, Montreat, for their faithful witness to the gospel. A church body that loves God's word as an active agent has a way of always asking questions that push to the heart of affective faith. Special thanks go to Richard White and Chad Smith for encouragement through the word proclaimed. Also, Edward Brouwer, Robert Sulaski and David Phillips were just foolish enough to ask questions about this project, just wise enough to tell me when I was missing something, and just faithful enough to keep asking. Thank you, brothers.

Finally, I especially thank my wife, Ann, whose whole-hearted support, tireless proofreading, and sharp theological mind spurred me on to persevere when I would have given up otherwise. Above all, I thank my Heavenly Father, who set me free to run toward the greater beauty of his son Jesus Christ.

Adam Newcomb Boyd
Black Mountain, NC
Spring 2019

Contents

Acknowledgements	i
Introduction	1
The Problem	1
Glossary	5
Where We Are Going And Why We Are Going There	7
Research Methodology	9
Summary	10
Chapter 1 — The Biblically Affected Heart	11
The Patriarch's Affection	12
The Deliverer's Affection	18
The King's Affection	24
The Prophet's Affection	31
God's Comprehensive Beauty	32
God's Essential Beauty	33
God's Active Beauty	35
The Savior's Affection	37
The Pharisee's Affection	44
Peter's Affection	49
John's Affection	52
Chapter Summary	55
Chapter 2 — Beauty, Sensation, and the Affected Heart	57

Two Faculties of the Mind	59
The Primacy of the Heart	60
Signs of Holy Affection	62
First Sign: The New Sense	63
Second Sign: Lack of Self Interest	66
Third Sign: Love of His Moral Excellency	68
Fourth Sign: The Enlightened Mind	69
Fifth Sign: Effectual Conviction	71
Sixth Sign: Evangelical Humility	73
Seventh Sign: A Changed Nature	77
Eighth Sign: A Spirit of Love and Meekness	79
Ninth Sign: An Increasingly Softened Heart	80
Tenth Sign: Symmetry of Virtues	81
Eleventh Sign: Increasing Desire	84
Twelfth Sign: Christian Practice	86
The Cause of Changed Affections	89
Suffering	91
Two Operations of Faith	94
Sensation and Beauty	96
The Christian Sermon	96
Consent to Being	97
Chapter Summary	101
Chapter 3 — Our Context and the Affected Heart	**103**
Stoddard's Influence	104
Jonathan Edwards's Foundations	107
Philosophical Foundations	109
Locke	109
A Few Words on "Sinners"	112
Newton	114
Other Cultural Changes	117
A Rising Generation	119
Family Tensions	121
Imperfect Solutions	122

Our Cultural Context 124
    Modern and Postmodern 125
    What Is/Was The Emergent Church? 128
    Another Take 131
    Emergents and the Bible 135
    And Now This 138
    Edwards and the Bible 141
Edwards's Response to Modernism 143
A Case Study in Application 146
Chapter Summary: Back to the Bigger Picture 148

Chapter 4 — A Model for Application   151
An Age of Opportunity 152
    Urgency 153
    Opportunity 155
Week One: Introduction 157
    Jesus and His Parents 158
    Anthropology 160
    Why Did We? 162
Week Two: A Tale of Two Prophets 163
    Balaam 164
    Isaiah 166
    How Do We Get It? 168
    Why Did We? 171
Week Three: In His Image 171
    Review 171
    Nicodemus 172
    How Does This Happen? 174
    Why Did We? 176
Week Four: Increasing Hunger 177
    Adam Exposed 178
    Moses 180
    Why Did We? 185
Week Five: Lack of Self Interest 185

    Jacob 191
    How Did It Come To This? 192
    Just Like Us 194
    How Do We Change? 195
    Why Did We? 197
  Chapter Summary 198

Conclusion   199
  The Cosmic Yawn 201
  The Need 202
  The Solution 202
  Recommendations 204

Bibliography   209

Index   215

Introduction

The Problem

ABOUT FIFTEEN YEARS AGO I was left speechless by the honesty of a seventeen year old girl. Caroline was a Counselor in Training (CIT) at the summer camp where I served as director. She started with us when she was nine and for eight summers her faith development was a central focus of some of our best staff. So one midsummer afternoon I was happy to find her by the dock during free-swim where I could ask how her faith was being challenged in her new position as a CIT. I expected to hear of a young but growing commitment to Christ. Instead she responded that she "believed" everything she had been taught about the gospel, she was convinced it was all true, but that if she were honest she really did not care that much about it. Caroline continued to say that she was more excited about an upcoming cheerleading camp and the possibility of spending more time with friends from school than she was about God's love, the great commission, the means of grace, or the resurrection of Christ. For Caroline those things were true, but they were not relevant to her day to day life. It was not surprising that Caroline felt this way. She was seventeen, after all, and very much involved in the opportunities that her quick mind and winsome social skills made available. What was surprising was her honesty.

Three weeks ago I had a similar conversation with one of my favorite senior staff members. Now twenty-four, and recently married, Mary Page grew up in what I hope was a thoughtful Christian home (mine, actually), is an active member of an evangelical, reformed church, and is committed to the truth of Scripture. Frankly, she is exactly who you would hope your daughter would become, and I have grown to respect her opinion enough to listen carefully when she describes her values, and those of her friends. When I asked about how younger evangelicals felt about the current social flashpoints she affirmed her dependence on the Bible and then said that beliefs that include people feel right and those that exclude people feel wrong. She did not state these as rules, but they were clearly a nudge in her hermeneutic.

Caroline was my first, and Mary Page my persistent, evidence that there was a change among younger Christians. It is a change that has been a long time coming, a reaction to the priorities of our immediate evangelical past, and not all together bad. Caroline's disinterest was a reaction to what she experienced as a disconnected orthodoxy. To her, the faith felt like a body of correct information that served little purpose in the immediate world and so she expressed what is now increasingly described as a desire for authenticity. Mary Page's inclusive gentleness was a more mature reaction to the same. It was also a search for a middle way between a settled theological confidence and an explosion of cultural openness. As Robert Webber has asked, "What will reach these youth and draw them into faith (or a healthy faith)? The Pragmatist's (earlier generation) bywords were 'big,' 'flashy,' 'slick,' 'entertaining,' and 'What's in it for me?' The younger evangelical's bywords are 'real,' 'genuine,' 'relational,' 'honest,' 'mix it up,' and 'What can I do for others?'"[1] The more recent words are authenticity, relevance, generosity and inclusion.

---

[1] Robert E. Webber, *The Younger Evangelicals* (Grand Rapids, MI: Baker Books, 2002), 46.

INTRODUCTION

The problem with the pragmatist's and younger evangelical's lists is not with the things included but rather those that were excluded, and by these exclusions we find a hint at what the younger evangelicals mean by "authentic" faith. Specifically, many are defining their faith in terms of self-attesting intuition. At the same time people like Caroline find that older evangelicals have defined their faith in terms of right belief, and sadly, a greater love for being correct than for Christ Himself. Mary Page might say, a greater love for being correct than for others. This correctness is a careful, beautiful idol that becomes more hidden each time it is polished. Scripture, on the other hand, speaks to both in one voice: we are built for experience and truth. "And now, Israel, what does the LORD your God require of you, but to fear the LORD your God, to walk in all his ways, to love him, to serve the LORD your God with all your heart and with all your soul" (Deut 10:12).

Unfortunately, the younger evangelicals' desire for honesty and authenticity often takes the form of a protest movement. A decade ago it was given a clear voice by the leaders of the Emergent Church Movement. As D. A. Carson described,

> It is difficult to gain a full appreciation of the distinctives of the movement without listening attentively to the life-stories of its leaders. Many of them have come from conservative, traditional, evangelical churches, sometimes with a fundamentalist streak. Thus the reforms that the movement encourages mirror the protests of the lives of many of its leaders.[2]

It has also been given a sturdy frame in the increasing popularization of postmodern ideas and, in particular, in an experiential epistemology. This is not to say that postmodernism is all bad, or even all that new (and maybe not even post), but rather that many of the

[2] D. A. Carson, *Becoming Conversant With the Emergent Church* (Grand Rapids, MI: Zondervan, 2005), 14.

recent theological trends among younger church leaders have risen in response to postmodern values. Similarly, emergent church leaders might argue that the priorities of other evangelicals (those Webber describes as "pragmatics") are a response to modern worldview values. In other words, the current cultural shift has highlighted weakness in both positions.

Biblical faith, however, is the product of the mind of God and so it stands alone, offensive to portions of every culture. As a result, elements of this faith are periodically obscured by particular cultures and philosophical schemes, and so a healthy biblical faith requires insight beyond that available to any particular cultural moment. It is a premise of this book that times of cultural transition, when a shift from one worldview to another has built a significant momentum, can provide an especially helpful perspective since each critique of the other reveals its own resistance to biblical faith.

One such time was the mid-eighteenth century. As the outworking of the Enlightenment reached across the Atlantic, divisions emerged similar to those we see today among evangelicals. In particular, the life and writings of Jonathan Edwards demonstrate a need to define the relationship between authentic experience and right belief. As Stephen Stein notes in his forward to Conrad Cherry's work on Edwards,

> In the 1740s Edwards struggled to define a theological position that embraced both the mind and the affections. He rejected the efforts of those who wanted to dismiss the widespread religious stirrings as the product of deluded imagination and manipulative ministers, declaring instead that the revivals represented the genuine work of God's spirit. At the same time he chided those driven by the awakenings to extreme ecstatic behavior and censori-

ousness calling rather for continued commitment to the principles of order and intellect.[3]

Edwards served as a pastor during a time when the church fluctuated between heightened emotions and spiritual deadness. Additionally, he wrote in the midst of a changing world. The colonies were becoming "America." The state would soon supplant the church and reason stood to challenge revelation. In the midst of this cultural transition Edwards argued that the greatest danger to biblical faith was not from the changing world but rather from counterfeits from within the church. According to Edwards the crux for the church in transition is that the distinguishing marks of biblical faith must be clearly understood and the most fundamental distinguishing mark is a change in affection founded on the independent beauty of God. The questions for today are how can a Christian leader facilitate change in affection, and how can we as Christians find Jesus increasingly beautiful?

Glossary

1. Affection: For Edwards, "Affection is a *felt* response to an object called forth by an *understanding* of the *nature* of the object..."[4] Affection is a capacity of the soul, endowed by God, and it may cause inclination or aversion in various degrees. The capacity for gracious affection, or true religious affection, requires regeneration by the Holy Spirit.

---

[3] Conrad C. Cherry, *The Theology of Jonathan Edwards, A Reappraisal*, Forward by Stephen J. Stein and new introduction by Conrad C. Cherry, 1990 (Bloomington and Indianapolis, IN: Indiana University Press, 1966), xii.

[4] Victor Shepherd, http://www.victorshepherd.on.ca/Course/Historical Theology/, access date, March 2, 2010.

2. Aesthetics: A branch of philosophy that examines the nature of beauty, art, and our response to each.[5]

3. Emergent Church: A broad movement that includes an emphasis on experiential, narrative driven, participatory faith and worship, and represents an effort to accommodate postmodernism within the bounds of Christianity.

4. Postmodernism: A reaction to modern epistemology that is applied broadly (literature, art, philosophy, music, etc.). It denies the existence of ultimate principles, or our access to them. Postmodernism refers to a "complex set of reactions to modern philosophy and its presuppositions, rather than to any agreement of substantive doctrines."[6]

5. Worldview: A "set of presuppositions (assumptions which may be true, partially true, or entirely false) which we hold (consciously or subconsciously, consistently or inconsistently) about the basic make up of our world."[7] As such, it is the standard used in assigning degrees of meaning and value to events or ideas and includes an idea of a highest good.

6. Younger Evangelicals: A subset of the broader evangelical movement that is influenced by postmodern and post 9/11 events.[8]

---

[5] Susan L. Feagin, "Aesthetics," *The Cambridge Dictionary of Philosophy* (Cambridge: Cambridge University Press, 1995), 10.

[6] Robert Audi, "Postmodernism," *The Cambridge Dictionary of Philosophy* (Cambridge: Cambridge University Press, 1995), 634.

[7] James W. Sire, *The Universe Next Door* (Downers Grove, IL: InterVarsity Press, 1997), 16.

[8] Webber, *The Younger Evangelicals*, 44.

INTRODUCTION

Where We Are Going And Why We Are Going There

This book is written to explore the qualities of a healthy, biblical faith. Much of Edwards's work on the nature and inclination of our affections is obscured by difficult language and culturally distant descriptions. The same is true regarding his work describing the object of our affection. Granted, there has been a good deal of secondary work done unpacking these ideas, but very little of it is accessible for the average Christian reader. Our primary command is to love the Lord our God with all our hearts. In considering the nature of our affections and the ideas of beauty that engage them, this book is written to develop the most foundational dynamic of our faith. In other words, we will look at both our love (affection) and our God (beauty). Something is broken about us; why else would we find Netflix more entertaining than worship? This is actually good news, because it means there is something more to our faith than we have yet experienced. This book is written to begin the healing process by looking at a biblical view of a renewed heart and rightly ordered affections.

We will know we have hit this mark if we accomplish four things. First, and always the best starting point, is to build a biblical/theological foundation (Chapter 1). Here we will explore the Bible's description of a redeemed, affected heart and the object of its affection. This is the foundation and the starting question is what does the Bible describe as ordinary Christian experience?

Second, we will consider the same as a historical/literature review (Chapter 2). The question is how has the church done this, and in particular, what is so valuable in Edwards's approach? However, because of the large amount that Edwards wrote during his short life, and the even larger amount written as commentary, the primary focus of this project is limited to Edwards's 1746 *Treatise on Religious*

Affections. Other material will be considered, but this is the only of his writings intended to be covered in significant detail.

Third is a bit of analysis (Chapter 3). This will be an evaluation of the problem in light of the biblical/theological findings (Chapter 1) and the historical/literature review (Chapter 2). Particular attention will be paid to the comparison between Edwards's immediate context and that of the contemporary church. To help structure this chapter we will consider the emergent church, its decline, and to a lesser degree some of the corresponding positions of more contemporary younger evangelicals (the Mary Pages of the world). However, this section is not intended to be a thorough critique of the emergent church, or the contemporary evangelical church. This is where things start to heat up because this is where we live every day. Then in Chapter 4 we are going to sum it up with a model for application. This is the stuff I generally skip when reading a book. Please don't. Everything else is just information until we start aiming it at people (and hopefully at ourselves first), so I hope you will have some faces in mind when you read this section.

This book is not designed to cover new theological ground. Rather, it is to serve as a reminder of the primacy of an affection (what we find most beautiful) and a tool for those equipping church leaders. The focus will be theological rather than philosophical, though some discussion of the philosophical background will be both helpful and unavoidable.

Finally, I like reading where an author went to school before I read a book. It sometimes gives a hint to where they are coming from and what they mean by the terms they use, but sometimes I am surprised. So to avoid surprises you should know that I began my research with the following assumptions.

1. The primacy and reliability of the Bible. Scripture declares itself (both Old and New Testaments) to be from God (God breathed) and its words cannot be broken.[9] As such it is the word of God

[9] John 10:35.

and authoritative not merely in the experience of believers but objectively and for all.

2. The power of the Holy Spirit. It is the Holy Spirit who affects change in the affections of the believer. He ordinarily operates through common means of grace and there is no real change apart from Him.

3. The value of church history. God is active in the church and is drawing history to a final conclusion. As such church history displays God's care for his people, the habits of our sin, and the consistent nature of each.

4. The important, though fallible, voice of culture. Christ calls us to love people. People are not ordinarily engaged apart from their world, and the world, as they experience it, is shaped by the culture in which they find themselves. Among the first commands in scripture is to bring order to the world. Each culture is the result of that effort. As we are broken by sin, so is our culture.

Research Methodology

This book is based on exegetical, theological and historical research. Data is collected from both primary and secondary sources. Primary sources are found in the Bible, the writings of Jonathan Edwards, and the writings of prominent leaders in the Emergent Church Movement. Secondary sources are found in commentaries on each.

Data concerning the biblical foundations are gathered through primary exegesis of biblical texts. Special care is given to consider passages in their original languages and with a view of their larger historical and canonical contexts. Secondary sources are also considered. Among these are sermons and other commentary Edwards may have made on the text considered.

Historical research methodologies are utilized for the study of Edwards's life and events leading up to his writing on religious affections. Stoddard's position on baptism receives particular attention, as do the similarities of the current condition of the church and that of the mid eighteenth-century American colonies.

Theological research includes the writings of Edwards himself as well as those who have written as commentary. The work of Ronald Delattre is especially important in this respect; he is a treasure. Theological research includes the writings of some of the leaders of the Emergent Church, the responses of several evangelical scholars and some more recent evaluations and iterations of this broadly open grouping of evangelical leaders.

Research was conducted primarily in Black Mountain, NC and significant use was made of the L. Nelson Bell Library at Montreat College. Other resources include inter-library loan available through my local library and periodic visits to the RTS libraries in Charlotte and Orlando. Finally, I took advantage of the resources available through the Internet with a special emphasis on the ALTA Periodical Index.

Summary

Sin has disordered our affections. Instead of being moved by God's beauty we are more easily moved by smaller things. This tendency is so common, and so hidden that each generation, and each believer, has to address it anew. The way that Jonathan Edwards addressed this in the mid-eighteenth century was exceptional for both its thoroughly biblical foundation and its enduring nature. As such, his *Treatise Concerning Religious Affections* provides an outline for addressing the disordered affections in our lives as well as in the contemporary church.

Chapter 1
The Biblically Affected Heart

Studying biblical characters to discover the ordinary Christian experience is dangerous business. We tend to reduce their lives to a series of lessons or examples. The problem is that each stands at a particular moment in redemptive history and so each plays a different part in the progress of redemption. Each had a unique context and a particular purpose. Their circumstances are exceptional. However, their behaviors are also iconic. At exceptional times the interaction of our hearts with our God is less covered, more evident. There is no margin to hide truth under distraction.

That said, establishing a biblical foundation for topics discussed in subsequent chapters must be the starting point. While Edwards provided voluminous scripture references for each of his arguments, he approached his topics with a systematic rather than a biblical/historical method. The purpose of this chapter is to begin with God's Word before we move to its systematic application.

The Patriarch's Affection

Jacob is the most approachable of the patriarchs. His younger brother status, undeserved blessing, and persistent conflict feel as familiar to modern readers as they are descriptive of the nation he fathered. Additionally, his narrative is central to the history of redemption. As Abraham was the father of the nation, Jacob was the "father of the tribes."[1] As such, we find in Jacob an exceptional calling and a familiar humanity, and in the meeting of these two we see something of the nature of the affected heart.

Having lost his family Jacob meets Rachel. Here again he goes to extreme measures to secure the thing he desires. The answer to why he does this may be found in 29:11–12. "Then Jacob kissed Rachel and wept aloud. And Jacob told Rachel that he was her father's kinsman...." This awkward kiss draws our minds to the last kiss described in Jacob's life.[2] "So he came near and kissed him. And Isaac smelled the smell of his garments and blessed him and said, 'See, the smell of my son is as the smell of a field that the LORD has blessed!" (Gen 27:27). The exceptional intimacy of this kiss intended for Esau was a sharp reminder of the family he had lost. Now, in the presence of his extended family, Jacob seeks from Rachel what he once sought from his father.

At this point the narrator goes a step further, noting that the years Jacob worked for Rachel "seemed to him but a few days because of the love he had for her" (Gen 29:20). As with the kiss, we are reminded of the last time this phrase was used. In fact, it was the exact phrase used by Jacob's mother in her description of how long he would hide before it would be safe to return to his family.

---

[1] Willem VanGemeren, *The Progress of Redemption* (Grand Rapids, MI: Academe Books, 1988), 103.

[2] Commentators also note that the word "kissed" (*Vayi sha k*) is used likely as a pun on the word "water" (*Vayash k*) used in v. 10. As the sheep thirst for water Jacob thirsts for family, each a matter of life and death.

Here is the heart of the matter. Jacob's desire for Rachel was built of the same stuff as his desire for his father's blessing. Even more noteworthy is that this love was so intense that it made any effort simple. In commenting on 1 Peter 1:8 Edwards notes that suffering shows and perfects our love.[3] Here, even after a remarkable vision of God at Bethel, Jacob's inordinate love is shown, and in a sense perfected. Sadly, we soon see that Rachel's love could no more "answer the expectation of the appetite"[4] than Isaac's stolen blessing. Thus, the stage is set for the central moment of Jacob's narrative, the birth of his children.

It is interesting that here at the structural center of Jacob's story the weight of the narrative is carried by his two wives. The result is to show the pattern of his inordinate love as common and infectious. As Isaac favored Esau over Jacob so Jacob favors Rachel over Leah. The hurt this causes is seen in the names of Leah's first four children.

> When the LORD saw that Leah was not loved, he opened her womb, but Rachel was barren. Leah became pregnant and gave birth to a son. She named him Reuben, for she said, "it is because the LORD has seen my misery. Surely my husband will love me now." She conceived again and when she gave birth to a son she said, "Because the LORD heard that I am not loved, he gave me this one too." So she named him Simeon. Again she conceived, and when she gave birth to a son she said, "Now at last my husband will become attached to me, because I have borne him three sons." So he was named Levi. She conceived again, and when she gave birth to a son she said, "This time I will praise the LORD." So she named him Judah. Then she stopped having children (Gen 29:31–35).

---

[3] WJE 2:93.

[4] WJE 2:379.

Perhaps as a hint of the healing to come, verse 29 is the first use of the covenant name of the LORD recorded since Jacob's meeting Laban nearly eight years previous.[5] Even so, Leah's naming her first three children in reference to her desire for Jacob's attention is remarkably similar to Jacob's extreme behavior in seeking his father's blessing. But, this changes with the naming of her fourth child. Here the name Judah (praise) stands without reference to Jacob, as her deeper affection appears to have been transferred to God. This is further supported by the last sentence noting that with this resolution she stopped having children. If Edwards is correct in saying that "the Author of the human nature has not only given affections to men, but has made 'em very much the spring of men's actions,"[6] then clearly there has been a change in affection. However, in keeping with the economy of the entire narrative, we are given very little detail about the mechanism for this change. The effect is beautiful, coaxing us further into Jacob's story by leaving us asking how it happened. We are given a glimpse into the answer three chapters later.

After concluding his conflict with Laban God calls Jacob to affirm his position as the covenant heir and finish the business with Esau (Gen 31:3). From the outset of chapter 32 we notice that there is something new happening, and that this new thing is both visible and spiritual in nature. The first verse tells us that the journey begins with Jacob receiving messengers from God. Then, in verse three he sends messengers of his own, and finally in verse six he receives messengers back. The interplay between God's messengers and Jacob's messengers highlights the uniquely spiritual element in Jacob's story.[7] The point is that more is going on here than meets the eye. In other words,

---

[5] There is something beautiful seen in the fact that it is the spurned wife, the least among the community, that reintroduces covenant intimacy to Jacob's circle. While Leah was not the beautiful wife she was the one who brought beauty. This feels central to the nature of Christian community.

[6] *WJE* 2:100.

[7] The same word, *Ma l achei* (messenger), is used in all three verses.

there is a subtle reference to a uniquely spiritual event, and while it is not clear whether this was evident to Jacob it is at least recognized by the narrator. It is a similar "spiritual sense" that Edwards describes as the foundational quality of authentic Christian experience.[8] It is important to note that this text leaves the modern reader's best questions unanswered. Specifically, how does the narrator recognize that the messengers are from God, and does Jacob recognize it at all? What is this spiritual sense, and how is it cultivated? For those questions we must turn to Edwards.

The account continues with what Walter Brueggerman describes as an extraordinary prayer and the first extended prayer found in Scripture.[9] Derek Kidner goes further, noting that the impending meeting with Esau stirs a "hunger awakened by the crisis, but not determined by it."[10] In other words, it is the anxiety surrounding the meeting that sets loose God's purpose for Jacob. Specifically, as Jacob prepares to confront the power of his brother, he finds himself attacked by the beauty of his God.

> And Jacob was left alone. And a man wrestled with him until the breaking of the day. When the man saw that he did not prevail against Jacob, he touched his hip socket, and Jacob's hip was put out of joint as he wrestled with him. Then he said, "Let me go, for the day has broken." But Jacob said, "I will not let you go unless you bless me." And he said to him, "What is your name?" And he said, "Jacob." Then he said, "Your name shall no longer be called Jacob, but Israel, for you have striven with God and with men, and have prevailed." Then Jacob asked

---

[8]*WJE* 2:197.

[9]Walter Brueggemann, *Genesis*. Interpretation. James L Mayes, ed. (Atlanta, GA: John Knox Press, 1982).

[10]Derek Kidner, *Genesis*. Tyndale Old Testament Commentaries (Downers Grove, IL: InterVarsity Press, 1967), 169.

him, "Please tell me your name." But he said, "Why do you ask me my name?" And there he blessed him (Gen 32:24–29).

Here, in just five verses (fifty-three words in the Hebrew), the narrator describes a life-changing encounter with the beauty of God. The encounter is one of power, change and mystery. It is where Edwards's new sense is literally beat into Jacob's life.

The context is important as this meeting is the result of Jacob's fear of Esau's power. Jacob's impassioned prayer, careful planning, and final decision to be alone the night before the meeting stand as evidence of this anxiety. Then, fretting at the prospect of standing before his brother's face,[11] Jacob finds himself before the face of God. As Kidner notes, it is here that Jacob discovers that "it was against Him (God), not Esau or Laban, that he had been pitting his strength."[12] Finally realizing this, Jacob abandons all other ambitions, even life itself, in hopes of holding the greater beauty. Now in place of his father's embrace Jacob holds God in his arms; in place of his father's blessing Jacob stakes his life for the blessing of his God. This change in ambition or, more basically, change in affection, is the ground for a more fundamental transformation. As Brueggemann explains, "That is how Israel comes on the horizon. Israel is not formed by success of shrewdness or land, but by an assault from God."[13]

Edwards notes, "All spiritual discoveries are transforming ... A man may be restrained from sin, before he is converted; but when he is converted, he is not only restrained from sin, his very heart and nature is turned ..."[14] It is this turning of nature that is in view in

---

[11] The word "face" is used 4 times (each as an idiom) in verse 20. Jacob begins the chapter living in reference to Esau's face and ends living in reference to God's, thus naming the place Peniel.

[12] Kidner, *Genesis*, 169.

[13] Brueggemann, *Genesis*, 269.

[14] *WJE* 2:340–41.

Jacob's re-naming. Until this point Jacob pursued blessing on his life, but he now pursues blessing against his life, even at the cost of his life. God's holiness is dangerous to Jacob, his assault threatening, but now, finally, also beautiful.

It should not be missed that it is when Jacob saw God being weak for him ("when the man saw he did not prevail against Jacob") that he was changed. Edwards might describe this by saying that it was God's limiting his natural attribute of power in deference to his moral attribute of grace that finally changed Jacob's heart.[15] Certainly this one who could cause a life-long injury to his hip with a mere touch could have overcome Jacob easily. If Edwards is correct in saying a "true love to God must begin with a delight in his holiness, not with a delight in any other attribute; for no other attribute is truly lovely without this,"[16] then it may be that it is here in God's holiness, his moral decision to limit his power, that Jacob finally finds God's presence more beautiful than his blessing.[17]

This experience of God's beauty, this intimacy of both relationship and revelation (remember, this finally happened when Jacob was alone), had a very particular result. Jacob wants more. He wants to bridge the gap; he wants self-disclosure. Recognizing God's beauty does not exhaust it and Jacob wants God himself. And so, Jacob asks for his name. Edwards contributed, "'Tis as much the nature of one that is spiritually new born, to thirst after growth in holiness as 'tis the nature of a newborn babe, to thirst after the mother's breast; who has the sharpest appetite, when he is best in health."[18] Finally, we find Jacob in his best health. Finally, we see the person we want to become.

---

[15] *WJE* 2:255.

[16] *WJE* 2:257.

[17] What Jacob sees at Peniel we see again at Golgotha.

[18] *WJE* 2:377.

But while God's beauty is revealed, it is still a dangerous mystery, and so he refused to give his name. At this point it becomes hard not to imagine Moses's thoughts as he recorded Jacob's request. Certainly, he would have remembered asking the same question, and been led to wonder that in his case God would answer.

The Deliverer's Affection

Jacob is to Jamestown (the beginning) as Moses is to Trenton (the crisis). Further, as crossing the Delaware rested on an apparent miracle, crossing the Red Sea required an actual miracle. In each case the nation is shaped by both its beginning and its moment of crisis. For Moses, the crisis is brought to an early climax with the crossing of the Red Sea; it is here that he pauses to record his song of thanksgiving (Ex 15:1–21).

While these verses are recognized as some of the oldest poetry in the Bible, there is little agreement among commentators as how best to understand their structure. Terence Fretheim sees Moses's and Miriam's songs as two separate pieces, put together by a later editor. He believes Miriam's song is primary, with Moses's being a later expansion. He writes, "In terms of the present redaction, however, the Song of Miriam functions as an antiphon, serving to reinforce the thanksgiving voiced by the people as a whole."[19] I would go a step further saying that the two should be read as a single literary unit, originally performed and placed together with a clear arrangement and purpose. As such they might be structured as follows:

> A Stanza 1 (1–5): Sing: horse and rider are thrown into the sea
> > B Stanza 2 (6–10): Your greatness, majesty and power defeat your enemy

[19] Terence E. Fretheim, *Exodus. Interpretation* (Louisville, KY: John Knox Press, 1991), 161.

> C Stanza 3 (11–13): Who is like you?
> B Stanza 4 (14–18): The people tremble because
> they have heard of your power over your enemy
> A Stanza 5 (21): (The Women's Choir brings it home)
> Sing: the horse and rider are thrown into the sea

If this structure is reasonable then verses 11–13 bear the weight of the narrator's focus.

> Who is like you, majestic in holiness, awesome in glorious deeds, doing wonders? You stretched out your right hand; the earth swallowed them. You have led in your steadfast love the people whom you have redeemed; you have guided them by your strength to your holy abode.

In these verses we find two emphases, both in reference to God's holiness. The first is the obvious description of God's character as holy in the sense that he is distinct from other powers (who is like you?).[20] Second, this distinction is demonstrated by what Edwards would describe as the moral excellencies of his holiness, namely his "steadfast love" and remarkable presence (holy abode). This first point is supported by John Durham who describes Pharaoh as mocked by his own staccato boasting in verse 9 (I will pursue, I will overtake, I will divide the spoil, I will draw my sword).[21] In this sense there is a facet of separateness or distinction in the narrator's use of holiness, but it is the second emphasis, his steadfast love and presence, or the moral dynamic of his holiness, that is at the heart of this book. The result is that we are left asking, what kind of beauty is this?

Here, at the center of Israel's redemptive history, and the structural center of Moses's song celebrating that moment, God's glory is seen

---

[20] Isn't this the question we asked when God limited his power at Peniel, and isn't it the question we should ask at the cross? What kind of God would save this way?

[21] John I. Durham, *Exodus*. Word Biblical Commentary. (Dallas, TX: Word Books Publishers, 1987), 207.

in his available presence and steadfast love. Before they are given the law, before they are given a form of worship, they are given a reason to worship. They are called to worship not so that they will be redeemed, but because they already are redeemed; not so that they will have their God's blessing, but because they already have that blessing. The point is that worship is founded on the beauty of God as demonstrated in his moral holiness (redeeming, steadfast love) rather than as a means to approach the deity. This is the truest distinctive facet of God's holiness—it is the foundation of the Christian experience. They follow because he leads in love and because he has redeemed ("You have led in your steadfast love the people whom you have redeemed"). It is these qualities revealed that leaves us asking, what kind of God is this, or "Who is like you O LORD, among the gods?" (15:11). This is the ongoing Christian question and we are exhorted to ask it over and over, in every devotion, in every service and in every prayer.

It may be argued that I am reaching too far here; that the people are worshiping because of the immediate relief of their rescue from Egypt. You saved our bacon, we like you. But the crux issue here is the order. It is not 1) worship God; 2) get salvation benefits (God's redeeming love). It is the reverse. The gospel is always the reverse. Indeed, I would go further saying that the Israelites' redemption, seen in their rescue from the Egyptians, demonstrates God's beauty more than his utility, and it is this beauty that is the real prize. As Jacob held on to God at the risk of his life, God's people will worship him regardless of any benefit to theirs.[22] His salvation is more a demonstration of his beauty than his usefulness. His beauty is the thing.[23]

---

[22] cf. *WJE* 2:240.

[23] Being a Christian is not about being saved. It is not even about being good or being on God's side. It is about finding something so beautiful that you cannot live without it. And so church, show us his beauty!

THE BIBLICALLY AFFECTED HEART

This is well seen in Exodus 33. Here we find that God has rescued his people, he has given the law, and the people have worshiped the calf. Then, in verse 3, he makes a remarkable offer. God will send a messenger before them (reminding us of Jacob sending messengers ahead to clear the way with Esau). This messenger will fight their battles, secure the land, and fulfill the covenant promises. His reason is reasonable; they are a stiff necked people and his holy presence would be a danger. Indeed, the danger stabs at the heart of God's promise to Abraham (v. 1). How could he give them the land or multiply their descendants if he is forced to "consume (them) on the way" (v. 3)?

Tim Keller has noted that what Israel saw as the "disastrous word" (v. 4) might be viewed by many as the perfect religion. It is all of the blessing (God's utility) without the messiness of an awkwardly present God (God's dangerous beauty). It is the car keys without the curfew. They get the land (milk, honey, etc.), they get the descendants ("to you and your offspring I will give it") but they lose God's presence. It is everything except the beauty.

At this point the narrative changes. Verses 7–11 seem to leave the current story to describe another event all together:

> [7]Now Moses used to take the tent and pitch it outside the camp, far off from the camp, and he called it the tent of meeting. And everyone who sought the LORD would go out to the tent of meeting, which was outside the camp. [8]Whenever Moses went out to the tent, all the people would rise up, and each would stand at his tent door, and watch Moses until he had gone into the tent. [9]When Moses entered the tent, the pillar of cloud would descend and stand at the entrance of the tent, and the LORD would speak with Moses. [10]And when all the people saw the pillar of cloud standing at the entrance of the tent, all the people would rise up and worship, each

> at his tent door. ¹¹Thus the LORD used to speak to Moses face to face, as a man speaks to his friend (Ex 33:7-11).

It is a fascinating and important paragraph but it seems so out of place that many wonder at its purpose in the story. Fretheim suggests helpfully that it builds suspense by slowing the action of the narrative.[24] Perhaps, but more importantly, it shows the life with God that the people experienced as ordinary. Specifically, God's beauty is shown in his gracious stooping to give his evident presence. "Thus the LORD used to speak to Moses face to face, as a man speaks to a friend" (v. 11). The point is that God's beauty is seen in his graciously dwelling with his people and seeing this is what leads the nation to worship/love/demonstrate affection.

Now, having given this background, the narrator returns to the problem at hand.

> ¹³Now therefore, if I have found favor in your sight, please show me now your ways, that I may know you in order to find favor in your sight. Consider too that this nation is your people." ¹⁴And he said, "My presence will go with you, and I will give you rest." ¹⁵And he said to him, "If your presence will not go with me, do not bring us up from here. ¹⁶For how shall it be known that I have found favor in your sight, I and your people? Is it not in your going with us, so that we are distinct, I and your people, from every other people on the face of the earth?" (Ex 33:13–16).

Moses asks for and receives a promise of God's continuing presence (they are his people after all, v. 13), and then, like Abraham pleading for Sodom, pushes further. God's promise is for Moses ("my presence will go with you, and I will give you rest" v. 15), and Moses wants to be very clear that it is for the people, too. Where God speaks of "you"

---

[24] Fretheim, *Exodus*, 295.

(v. 15) Moses speaks of "us" (v. 16). This view of God's beauty is then not reserved for the leader but is to be the experience of the ordinary believer.

God's beauty will be available for all his people, but again Moses asks for more.

> [18] Moses said, "Please show me your glory." [19] And he said, "I will make all my goodness pass before you and will proclaim before you my name 'The LORD.' And I will be gracious to whom I will be gracious, and will show mercy on whom I will show mercy. [20] But," he said, "you cannot see my face, for man shall not see me and live" (Ex 33:18-20).

Moses asks to see God's glory and God answers by saying that his mercy, his goodness, his moral holiness is his glory. God's beauty is his character, and specifically, his moral holiness. As Edwards describes it, believers "love divine things primarily for their holiness: they love God, in the first place, for the beauty of his holiness or moral perfection as being supremely amiable in itself."[25]

It is also interesting that his goodness is somehow "viewed" propositionally. Words, here the words of God, create sensation. Specifically, God's words are "viewed" as a description of his character, a proclamation. Again, Edwards might respond saying, "Holy affections are not heat without light; but evermore arise from some information of the understanding..."[26] Regardless, God's answer to Moses is a description of his character. God's character, his moral holiness, is his beauty and access to this is the purpose of our faith.

---

[25] *WJE* 2:256.

[26] *WJE* 2:266.

The King's Affection

If Jacob was the father of the tribes, and Moses their leader in crisis, then David was their king in victory. His reign represents the pinnacle of the nation's power even as David's life is alternately threatened and made secure. As such he is the subject of the longest and most detailed biography in the Old Testament, and like Jacob and Moses, the Bible gives an important picture of David's interior, religious life. Here again it is important to note that David's circumstances were exceptional, but his emotional response is common as skin. We experience our lives as stories, biographies moving from one chapter to another. And so the chapters of David's story, moving from young shepherd to political outcast, from powerful king to stumbling father, feels real. As a result, David is someone from whom we are willing to learn. That his psalms have been at the heart of Christian worship since they were first penned stands as proof that his exceptional circumstances lay bare the most felt and important elements of our faith. Psalm 27 is a particularly poignant example.

In understanding Psalm 27 it is important to take note of its clear literary division. Specifically, verses 1-6 are so different from 7–14 that many struggle to explain their relationship to one another.[27] Regardless, the compiler of Psalms understood the two sections as related and best read/sung together. As such, they might be understood as a declaration followed by the application.

> The LORD is my light and my salvation; whom shall I fear? The LORD is the stronghold of my life; of whom shall I be afraid? ²When evildoers assail me to eat up my flesh, my adversaries and foes, it is they who stumble

---

[27] As Delitzsch exlains, "The two halves are very unlike one another... in ver. 7, the style becomes heavy and awkward, the strophic arrangement obscure, and even the boundaries of the lines of the verses uncertain; so that one is tempted to regard vers. 7–14 as the appendage of another writer" (1867:355).

and fall. ³Though an army encamp against me, my heart shall not fear; though war arise against me, yet I will be confident. ⁴One thing have I asked of the LORD, that will I seek after: that I may dwell in the house of the LORD all the days of my life, to gaze upon the beauty of the LORD and to inquire in his temple. ⁵For he will hide me in his shelter in the day of trouble; he will conceal me under the cover of his tent; he will lift me high upon a rock. ⁶And now my head shall be lifted up above my enemies all around me, and I will offer in his tent sacrifices with shouts of joy; I will sing and make melody to the LORD.

⁷Hear, O LORD, when I cry aloud; be gracious to me and answer me! ⁸You have said, "Seek my face." My heart says to you, "Your face, LORD, do I seek." ⁹Hide not your face from me. Turn not your servant away in anger, O you who have been my help. Cast me not off; forsake me not, O God of my salvation! ¹⁰For my father and my mother have forsaken me, but the LORD will take me in. ¹¹Teach me your way, O LORD, and lead me on a level path because of my enemies. ¹²Give me not up to the will of my adversaries; for false witnesses have risen against me, and they breathe out violence. ¹³I believe that I shall look upon the goodness of the LORD in the land of the living! ¹⁴Wait for the LORD; be strong, and let your heart take courage; wait for the LORD! (Ps 27:1–14).

Perhaps the division is better seen when we simply ask to whom is David speaking. The use of the first person in verses 1-6 and 13-14 suggest that this is self-talk, a way of reminding himself what he knows to be true. Verses 7-12 however, are clearly addressed to God; they are a prayer. Verses 1-6 are information, but the prayer of 7-12 is applied information. They represent time spent with the Father: it is not finding God useful in theory; it is experiencing him beautiful in practice. There is an intimacy (v. 10) that is as real as the slander and physical threat standing immediately before him (v. 2-3).

Also in this prayer we see the quality of this relationship. In verse 8, David is seeking the one thing that was denied to Jacob and Moses, to see God's face.[28] Here, like the two before him, David is reaching for God's presence rather than his help. In the midst of the danger he faces, David wants one thing from this dangerous God. He desires God for his immediate beauty.[29] It is interesting that David is seeking God's face in response to his command (which was not the case with Jacob or Moses), and that it is his "heart" that rises in obedience. As it is used here the heart speaks of the entire inner self and so as Elwell notes it is "from the heart one speaks to God (Ps 27:8)."[30] In other words, God has commanded David to seek an immediate experience of his presence and David responds from the desire of his whole inner self, not an isolated act of the will. As Edwards would note, the will is moved by its affection; one can not be moved without the other, and trying is the mistake of many "Christian" movements. Additionally, this presence, this reserved relationship, is described as astoundingly real. In verse 10 David says, "For my father and my mother have forsaken me, but the LORD will take me in." The most basic, felt and first love we know might finally be false in comparison with the reality of God's protective love. As Alter writes "The extravagance of this declaration of trust in God, perhaps the most extreme in the whole Bible, is breathtaking, and perhaps even disturbing."[31] This is not mere information about God. This is praise in the face of the reality

---

[28] These three together illustrate the progressive nature of revelation.

[29] This is the incredibly bold, almost irreverent desire of a quickened believer. What kind of God would dare us to act on this desire?

[30] Walter A. Elwell, *Baker Encyclopedia of the Bible,* Vol. 1 (Grand Rapids, MI: Baker Book House 1988), 939.

[31] Robert Alter, *The Book of Psalms* (New York: W.W. Norton & Company 2007). 93.

of his beauty. This is unlike anything else in human experience. This is what Caroline needed. This is what we need.

Returning to the first division, at the center of David's declaration (1-6) we find the crux of the matter: David's one thing. Specifically, David desires to gaze upon the beauty of the Lord. At first this verse seems out of place. In it David interrupts his description of the great danger of his enemies to declare his greater desire for his savior. Alter notes that verse 4 is relevant to the context in that the temple is within the security of the city walls, and was itself a place of political refuge.³² Even so, more than temple security, David desires temple presence, and this presence is described as "beauty."³³ Here, in the midst of multiple enemies approaching from multiple directions (note the use of the plural: evildoers, adversaries, foes), David cuts through distractions and reminds himself of a singleness of purpose.³⁴ As Edwards explains, trials "tend to refine (true religion), and deliver it from those mixtures of that which is false, which impede it; that nothing may be left but that which is true.³⁵

Kidner sees David's singleness of purpose as the best answer to distracting fears.³⁶ But it seems instead that David is at pains to show that his single purpose is not the cause of his victory but the result of God's beauty. Psalm 27 is not a call to an act of will, adopting David's one thing, but rather an invitation to behold God's beauty, leading to a single desire. In the end, Psalm 27 shows viewing God's beauty is both the cause and the end of Christian experience. The point here is that the self giving that Jacob and Moses desired in asking to see the

---

³²Ibid., 92.

³³נעם—agreeable, pleasant, lovely. Proverbs 3:17 "Her ways are ways of pleasantness, and all her paths are peace."

³⁴Every Christian sermon should be a reminder of one thing. David is prescribing Christian redundancy.

³⁵*WJE* 2:93.

³⁶Derek Kidner, *Psalms 1–72*. Tyndale Old Testament Commentaries (Downers Grove, IL: InterVarsity Press 1973), 121.

face of God is what David now describes as the ground of worship. Israel's story shows our need for God's face; Israel's worship shows the result.

In Psalm 63 we see David exploring the same theme, his desire for God himself, with a remarkably universal metaphor. As a result, Psalm 63 is among the best known and most loved of David's psalms. Speaking of this, and similar psalms, Delitzsch notes the universal quality, saying "They are inexhaustible, there always remains an undeciphered residue..."[37] Thus it is not a surprise to see that Edwards refers to Psalm 63 seven times in *Religious Affections,* second only to Psalm 119 for references cited. Even Artur Weiser, seldom noted for devotional over-statement, notes Psalm 63 as representing the "elemental yearning of a faithful heart."[38] It is this "elemental" characteristic of the psalm that makes it so helpful for this study.

Psalm 63 most likely describes David's wilderness exile during Absalom's rebellion. This is suggested by David's referring to himself as "the king" (v. 11), which could not have been a self-description during his earlier wilderness experiences. There is no pain more cutting than family pain, which explains why David's desire is so transparent; thus we see that David's great desire, his one thing, is his relationship with God.

David's opening phrase, "O God, you are my God" reveals an intimacy in relationship, a proprietary claim that borders on irreverent. As Kidner says, "The longing of these verses is not the groping of a stranger, the feeling of his way towards God, but the eagerness of a friend, almost a lover, to be in touch with the one he holds dear."[39]

---

[37] Franz Delitzsch, *Psalms.* Commentary on the Old Testament In Ten Volumes. Vol. 5 (Grand Rapids, MI: Wm B. Eerdman's Publishing Company, Reprint 1988), 212.

[38] Artur Weiser, *The Psalms.* The Old Testament Library (Philadelphia, PA: Westminster Press, 1962), 454.

[39] Kidner, *Psalms 1–72,* 224.

These few words, just two in the Hebrew,[40] convey a sense of reality that goes well beyond an idealistic musing. David is not speaking about information, he is speaking about an intimacy that is the result of having "looked upon" and "beholding" God's beauty, or "glory and power" (v. 2).

Psalm 63 is exceptional in the boldness of its claim of David's access to God. It is equally exceptional in the brute physicality of its metaphor:

> O God, you are my God; earnestly I seek you; my soul thirsts for you; my flesh faints for you, as in a dry and weary land where there is no water. ²So I have looked upon you in the sanctuary, beholding your power and glory. ³Because your steadfast love is better than life, my lips will praise you. ⁴So I will bless you as long as I live; in your name I will lift up my hands. ⁵My soul will be satisfied as with fat and rich food, and my mouth will praise you with joyful lips, ⁶when I remember you upon my bed, and meditate on you in the watches of the night (Ps 63:1–6).

As if to underscore the point, Robert Alter suggests that "soul" in verse one is better translated "throat" in deference to its parallel to "flesh."[41] While *nephesh* can certainly be translated this way, doing so obscures the more basic metaphor of the condition of our soul apart from God. Regardless, the same argument could be made in reference to verse five, where the parallel with lips is as strong, but again, the more important point would be lost. David does not want to eat rich foods, or drink clean water; he is instead describing a longing that is even more necessary for living, and even more more difficult to describe. David's point in using the word "soul" for throat is to show

---

[40]אלהים אלי

[41]Alter, *The Book of Psalms*, 216.

that his spiritual desire is more real, more felt, than physical pain. This desire for God himself is our most foundational desire. We are so bound by the rules of physics and biology that we tend to treat them as ultimate. Here, David is saying that they are not. Just as there is physicality to our lives there is also spirituality. Edwards would go further still, saying that the first evidence of authentic love for God is an experience of this "spiritual sense" as real. It is spiritually, then, that we perceive God as beautiful apart from his immediate usefulness.

For the Christian, this spiritual sense is more fundamental than the most basic physical qualities of thirst and hunger, or as we saw in Psalm 27, the love of God is more real than the most basic love we know otherwise, that of our mother. Both, however, are more difficult to describe and so we are left to wade in metaphor. The lone exception, the clearest statement, is found in verse three where we are told simply that God's love is better than life. More desirable than all that life offers, even than its most basic needs (food and water) is the love of God. Here is the deposed king, in a dry and weary land, in a place of "sun-burnt aridity and a nature that bears only one uniform ash-colored tint," longing for God's love above the restoration of anything he has lost.[42] The implication is that all the world offers leaves us thin and dying apart from the beauty of God. Today's metaphor might be a child playing his video game to the exclusion of food. After a while weakness will set in, finally leading to death.

In this way, as king, David stood as a type of Christ, seeking his father's presence both in the temple and in the wilderness. Almost 300 years later we find another finding that presence in the Temple built by David's son.

---

[42] Delizsch, *Psalms*, 215.

The Prophet's Affection

In the year that King Uzziah died I saw the Lord sitting upon a throne, high and lifted up; and the train of his robe filled the temple. ²Above him stood the seraphim. Each had six wings: with two he covered his face, and with two he covered his feet, and with two he flew. ³And one called to another and said: "Holy, holy, holy is the LORD of hosts; the whole earth is full of his glory!" ⁴And the foundations of the thresholds shook at the voice of him who called, and the house was filled with smoke. ⁵And I said: "Woe is me! For I am lost; for I am a man of unclean lips, and I dwell in the midst of a people of unclean lips; for my eyes have seen the King, the LORD of hosts!" ⁶Then one of the seraphim flew to me, having in his hand a burning coal that he had taken with tongs from the altar. ⁷And he touched my mouth and said: "Behold, this has touched your lips; your guilt is taken away, and your sin atoned for. ⁸And I heard the voice of the Lord saying, "Whom shall I send, and who will go for us?" Then I said, "Here am I! Send me." ⁹And he said, "Go, and say to this people:'" Keep on hearing, but do not understand; keep on seeing, but do not perceive.' ¹⁰Make the heart of this people dull, and their ears heavy, and blind their eyes; lest they see with their eyes, and hear with their ears, and understand with their hearts, and turn and be healed." ¹¹Then I said, "How long, O Lord?" And he said: "Until cities lie waste without inhabitant, and houses without people, and the land is a desolate waste, ¹²and the LORD removes people far away, and the forsaken places are many in the midst of the land. ¹³And though a tenth remain in it, it will be burned again, like a terebinth or an oak, whose stump remains when it is felled." The holy seed is its stump (Isa 6:1–13).

It might be argued that Isaiah is the chief among prophets, and that Isaiah 6 is the chief among his visions. Isaiah certainly records these events in a place and way that forms a literary hinge or transition as he both concludes the introductory material of chapters 1–5 and introduces the specifics of the rest of the book. The placement describes his vision in a way that demonstrates that God's holiness is the beginning and the end, the starting point and conclusion of ministry. Moreover, chapter 6 presents the "lived out" truth of the promises of chapters 1–5[43] as the word given to the nation are proven true in the life of the individual.[44] If the question is how a Christian leader can facilitate change in affection that is driven by the beauty of God then at some point we must discover how to move from the general idea of his beauty to a particular, personal, experience of it. These verses are an example of this happening.

God's Comprehensive Beauty

We tend to treat the historical background of a text as a lens to help discover the theological nugget that is our real interest. But here history is the nugget, and in this we see the comprehensive nature of God's beauty. The point is that God's purposes are both geopolitical and individual; for Isaiah there is no distinction. As such the political alliances, intrigue and drama are not the canvas on which God paints his beauty, or even the brush that he uses as a tool, but in a sense they are the paint, the medium itself. This is what is so elegantly communicated in the careful dating of verse 1. King Uzziah's death ended a long reign and "orderly co-regency" (partnered with Jotham) which had provided remarkable political stability in

---

[43] Specifically 1:16–19, 2:1–4 and 4:2–6.

[44] John N. Oswalt, *The Book of Isaiah Chapters 1–39*. The New International Commentary on the Old Testament (Grand Rapids, MI: Wm. B. Eerdmans Publishing, Co., 1986), 175.

the southern kingdom.[45] Concurrently, the northern kingdom (Israel) was enduring a long, unstable and divided monarchy. During this time one ruler (Menahem) willingly served as a vassal of Assyria and the other (Pekah) strained against the weakening Assyrian rule. The fractured political structures led to weakened economic conditions that in turn drove a breakdown in social justice. This was the time of Amos and Hosea ("Let justice roll down like waters, and righteousness like an ever-flowing stream," Amos 5:24). In all this Isaiah calls the nation(s) to trust in God rather than their own political efforts. It is difficult to see this and not be reminded of Jacob's scheming to steal the blessing that he had been promised since birth. As Watts has noted, "A drama normally develops a plot. So does the Vision."[46] This plot, the largest events of history, along with our responses to them, builds throughout Isaiah to finally demonstrate the beauty of God. By this I mean that his beauty is seen in both the most general, universal sense, and as Isaiah learns in the temple, the most specific, particular sense. As Isaiah announces nation-wide judgment he also describes a single sinner being healed. The ideal is particularized.

This is driven home in the first line of the chapter: "In the year that King Uzziah died I saw the Lord...." Coupled with the largest geopolitical event of the region is an abrupt use of the first person. Isaiah's personal experience of the holiness of God welded to God's activity in history.

God's Essential Beauty

God's presence unmistakably dominates the scene as the king is seated and the seraphim stand over ready to serve. And, their service is unique. As one commentator has noted, they are all wings and voice, ready for service and praise. It is noteworthy that the seraphim cover

---

[45] John D. W. Watts, *Isaiah 1–33*. Word Biblical Commentary (Waco, TX: Word Books 1985), 10.

[46] Ibid., li.

their faces, not daring to look on the beauty of God. This is especially interesting since we have noted that it is the movement of redemptive history from Jacob, to Moses, to David, to allow us this very view (finally realized in Jesus: "For God, who said, 'Let light shine out of darkness,' has shone in our hearts to give the light of the knowledge of the glory of God in the face of Jesus Christ" 2 Cor. 4:6). And so, the seraphim cover their faces, not because of their sin but because of God's glory.[47] Their covering of their "feet" may be euphemism for genitalia. Regardless, whether it is body, feet, or genitals, these mighty seraphim can not look on or be displayed before the creator. Even so, here stands Isaiah.

Verse 3 notes that the seraphim are calling to one another in what appears to be antiphonal singing or delighting with one another in the glory of God. Even in this incredibly personal, individual vision of God's glory we see that his beauty is experienced and expressed in community. In other words, an authentic affective experience is more than a merely individual experience. At the same time it is not less, and this is the crux point. Affective religious experience is comprehensive in the sense that it is both an individual and a community event.

Finally, the verbal element of the vision should not be overlooked. Oswalt notes, "The content of this experience is not merely numinous, emotive and nonrational. Had God only wished to convey his otherness to Isaiah that could have been done without words. But here the cognitive rational element is introduced."[48] In other words, affective religion is not merely an emotive touch but rather it is as accessible, concrete and ordinary as the words we use each day. There is content,

---

[47] See also 1 Peter 1:12 "It was revealed to them that they were serving not themselves but you, in the things that have now been announced to you through those who preached the good news to you by the Holy Spirit sent from heaven, things into which angels long to look."

[48] Oswalt, *The Book of Isaiah Chapters 1–39*, 179.

even content that describes God's essential otherness ("Holy, holy, holy").

Ordinarily when a word is doubled in Hebrew it means that something is a) superlative in the quality described, or b) possesses the quality described in its every part.[49] This sort of doubling conveys an intensity that is rare. The tripling of "Holy" on the other hand is unique. There is no other place in the Old Testament where this sort of tripling is found, just as there is no other place where we find a more direct description of God in his essence. Alec Motyer notes the exceptional quality of this description saying a "super-superlative has to be invented to express it (that there is none like God in this quality) and, furthermore, that this transcendent holiness is the total truth about God."[50] This is quite a statement: "the total truth about God." It drives home the point that Isaiah had an affective experience of God's presence that changed his life. At the center of that experience was God's holiness. Isaiah was not changed by a subjective experience. He was changed by the holiness of God as experienced in objective, cognitive, verbal revelation.

God's Active Beauty

Isaiah is a difficult book. Part of the reason for this is that it is so connected to what are now distant historical facts. Equally difficult is its conjunction and cycles of promises and curses. The effect, however, is to show God as "true to himself in mercy as he is in judgment."[51] In other words, as we see God perfect in justice we have evidence of his perfection in mercy. In light of the call to proclaim

---

[49] For example, when Genesis 14:10 wants to describe pits being everywhere, or perhaps their being big pits ("Now the Valley of Siddim was full of bitumen pits...") it literally says the valley was "pits pits."

[50] Alec J. Motyer, *Isaiah*. Tyndale Old Testament Commentaries (Downers Grove, IL: InterVarsity Press 1999), 81.

[51] Ibid., 77.

a devastating prophecy, one that is literally designed to justify even greater judgment (v. 10), Isaiah can continue forward in hope that as we see his judgment we will see his mercy.

Verses 8-10 seem designed to drive this home. They stand as a justification of God's judgment, and in this we see something remarkable. God sits on his throne, all powerful, but still beholden to his own moral beauty, his nature. He is always just and in this there is a terrible beauty, but it is still instructive in that it is God's nature to show his essence to his people. Referring to verse 10, Watts says that "as evangelists to bring the nations to repentance, the eighth-century prophets, indeed the great seventh-century prophets, were remarkably unsuccessful. This commission, given to Isaiah, insists that this was not their task."[52] It is, instead, their task to show God in his nature. Specifically, God's beauty, the very thing that affects our hearts, is seen in his acting consistently with both his justice and his mercy. This is his active beauty.

Finally, God's beauty is seen in what he values, or his aesthetic:

> Then I said, "How long, O Lord?" And he said: "Until cities lie waste without inhabitant, and houses without people, and the land is a desolate waste, [12]and the LORD removes people far away, and the forsaken places are many in the midst of the land. [13]And though a tenth remain in it, it will be burned again, like a terebinth or an oak, whose stump remains when it is felled." The holy seed is its stump (Isa 6:11–13).

Struck by the brutality of judgment Isaiah asks a pained question. How long will this go on? The answer is not encouraging. His judgment will be as complete as his nature is just, but so will his mercy. As dead as the tree is, there remains a stump, and it is not a memorial, but a seed. We are reminded, then, of God's faithful promise to

---

[52]Watts, *Isaiah 1–33*, 75

Abraham: that from his seed would come salvation, blessing to all the nations.

This is not Sunday School material. The full brutality of God's judgment is proof of his fidelity to his own nature. So to run past the judgment, to mitigate its force by describing its relief, will not do. An affecting vision of God includes his terrible beauty, his fearful justice, finally poured out on another tree on another hill.

The Savior's Affection

As we move into the New Testament we have the advantage of describing a culture with references and metaphors that is more familiar. First-century Jerusalem is simply easier for us to understand than that of the eighth century, B.C. Additionally, much of the New Testament, and in particular the gospels, is centered on a smaller geographical area with fewer political players, and those that are described have received much more attention in most churches. This is an advantage, but it is also a disadvantage. Familiarity with the stories and context tends to make us lazy. When Jacob names the place of his wrestling Peniel we are compelled to ask why, and even where. In asking these questions we go deeper into the Bible. It is a loss that we seldom feel compelled to ask the same questions in the New Testament.

In some ways Matthew 12 is an example of this. It is a familiar story, and with the exception of the description of the unpardonable sin, we generally read it confidently and quickly. Beginning in verse 12 Matthew tells of Jesus healing a demon-possessed man. The crowd responded appropriately, asking in effect if Jesus was the expected Messiah, or specifically "the Son of David." The Pharisees in turn respond by suggesting that Jesus' power over demons came from Satan himself. Jesus responds with a line that becomes the heading under which we must understand the rest of the chapter: "And if Satan casts out Satan, he is divided against himself. How then will his kingdom stand?" From there Jesus promises that blasphemy against the Spirit will not be forgiven. It is typical to tie these two events together. What we seldom do is read these verses in reference to those that follow.

> Either make the tree good and its fruit good, or make the tree bad and its fruit bad, for the tree is known by its fruit. [34]You brood of vipers! How can you speak good, when you are evil? For out of the abundance of the heart the mouth speaks. [35]The good person out of his good treasure brings forth good, and the evil person out of his evil treasure brings forth evil. [36]I tell you, on the day of judgment people will give account for every careless word they speak, [37]for by your words you will be justified, and by your words you will be condemned." [38]Then some of the scribes and Pharisees answered him, saying, "Teacher, we wish to see a sign from you." [39]But he answered them, "An evil and adulterous generation seeks for a sign, but no sign will be given to it except the sign of the prophet Jonah. [40]For just as Jonah was three days and three nights in the belly of the great fish, so will the Son of Man be three days and three nights in the heart of the earth. [41]The men of Nineveh will rise up at the judgment with this generation and condemn it, for they repented at the preaching of Jonah, and behold, something greater than Jonah is here (Mt 12:33–41).

In reference to a divided house Jesus describes blasphemy against the Spirit. In reference to a divided tree and a divided person (heart/tongue) Jesus describes the Pharisees' hearts (v. 33-34). And Jesus describes each as an impossibility. In fact, the entire chapter centers on the idea of division and unity. A person can not be divided in his actions and heart any more than a house can be divided against itself.

The idea of a person's heart is used only one time in the New Testament in a way that may refer to physical vitality (Lk 21:34). New

Testament writers more often followed the Old Testament use of the word heart, which is best understood as referring to the innermost part of a man.[53] This involves a) feelings, emotions, desires and passions, b) understanding, thought and reflection, c) will and the source of resolve, d) so "thus the heart is supremely the centre in man to which God turns, in which the religious life is rooted, which determines moral conduct."[54]

The point is that the New Testament idea of heart is as an integrating organ. It represents the whole self at its deepest root. There is then a one to one correlation between inclination and will, or desire and action, thus, "it is out of the abundance of the heart that the mouth speaks." William Hendriksen echoes this, "As a teeming population will overflow into adjoining territory, and a too full cistern into an overflow pipe, so the overplus of the heart will burst out into speech."[55] And so the healing of a demon-possessed man, a man who is internally himself plus another, is the right starting place for Jesus' discourse.

With this in mind we can come to the unforgivable sin, blasphemy against the Spirit, with a fuller context. As Hendriksen explains, "The Pharisees are ascribing to Satan what the Holy Spirit, through Christ, is achieving. Moreover, they are doing it willfully, deliberately."[56] In other words the Pharisees' words are a reflection of their hearts; they are evidence of their ontological composition. The issue is the nature of the speaker, not the words themselves. In fact, their nature has already been described as "evil" (7:11). These words are simply the ugly evidence.

---

[53] See for example 1 Samuel 16:7: "For the LORD sees not as man sees: man looks on the outward appearance, but the LORD looks on the heart."

[54] Johannes Behm, καρδία, *Theological Dictionary of the New Testament Vol. 3* (Grand Rapids, MI: Wm. B. Eerdmans Publishing, Co., 1966), 612.

[55] William Hendriksen, *Matthew.* New Testament Commentary (Grand Rapids, MI: Baker Book House, 1973), 530.

[56] Ibid., 529.

This is part of what Edwards describes in his seventh sign of gracious affection, specifically that it will always include a change of nature. He writes, "A swine that is of a filthy nature may be washed; but the swinish nature remains."[57] Just as there is no changing the pig, there was no changing the Pharisee, and so the chapter ends with the Pharisees again proving their lack of faith asking for a sign.

Next we come to chapter 22 where Jesus is again confronted by the Pharisees.

> But when the Pharisees heard that he had silenced the Sadducees, they gathered together. [35] And one of them, a lawyer, asked him a question to test him. [36] "Teacher, which is the great commandment in the Law?" [37] And he said to him, "You shall love the Lord your God with all your heart and with all your soul and with all your mind. [38] This is the great and first commandment. [39] And a second is like it: You shall love your neighbor as yourself. [40] On these two commandments depend all the Law and the Prophets (Mt 22:34–40).

In chapter 12 they had sent their disciples along with the Herodians, but this time they choose to question him directly. They are becoming more bold, perhaps desperate, less political. Verse 35 shows that it is a "lawyer," or expert in the law, who begins the questioning. As such he is an expert among experts and his question reflects his interest. Specifically, the question is which of the 613 laws of the Old Testament is the most important. Leon Morris notes that since there was no biblical yardstick to measure which was more important, any answer would open Jesus to criticism.[58] Jesus gave a very simple answer, which is perhaps noteworthy in such a complicated environment with so many politically charged alliances and differences in

---

[57] *WJE* 2:341.

[58] Leon Morris, *The Gospel According to Matthew* (Grand Rapids, MI: Wm. B. Eerdmans Publishing, Co., 1992) 563.

view (Sadducees, Pharisees, their disciples, Herodians, etc.). Jesus simply affirmed the entire law by quoting and expanding the Shema (Deut 6:5). This was the first text learned by every Hebrew child, and the fundamentally distinctive monotheistic confession establishing their nation as holy, apart from the polytheist in lands they would occupy. As much as any law could be, this was written on the heart of the nation.

That said, Jesus does not simply quote the Shema, he paraphrases it creating a commentary. Specifically, rather than quoting "Hear, O Israel: The LORD our God, the LORD is one. You shall love the LORD your God with all your heart and with all your soul and with all your might. And these words that I command you today shall be on your heart..." (Ex 6:4-5), Jesus replaces "strength" with "mind." While it is important to not read too much into this, it is still noteworthy. Hendriksen explains that the heart is "the hub of the wheel of man's existence, the mainspring of his thoughts, words and deeds." He continues that the soul is here used to mean the seat of emotional activity and the mind represents intellectual life as well as disposition and attitude.[59] The point is that Jesus is calling us to an engagement of our whole person.

Commenting on these verses, Edwards affirms the comprehensive nature of love: "The Scriptures do represent true religion, as being summarily comprehended in love, the chief of the affections, and fountain of all other affections."[60] He continues, "that this propensity or inclination of the soul, when in a sensible and vigorous exercise, becomes affection, and is no other than affectionate love" (107). However, Edwards also notes that love is not so "exclusive of habit" (107). His point is that habitual love, even carefully considered love, is the result of "disposition" or ontology.[61]

---

[59]Hendriksen, *Matthew*, 809.

[60]*WJE* 2:106.

[61]And this is the real question. How do we change the type of thing we are? How do we change what we love?

The point is that when asked about the most fundamental aspect of obedience and holiness Jesus describes the chief of all affections, love. Even more, he does so in a way that describes a tendency of the whole self (heart, soul, and mind). Jesus teaches that at the core of the faith is an authenticity, an integrated action of the whole person. As the author of Hebrews later notes, Jesus not only teaches this but also models it.

> Therefore, since we are surrounded by so great a cloud of witnesses, let us also lay aside every weight, and sin which clings so closely, and let us run with endurance the race that is set before us, ²looking to Jesus, the founder and perfecter of our faith, who for the joy that was set before him endured the cross, despising the shame, and is seated at the right hand of the throne of God. ³Consider him who endured from sinners such hostility against himself, so that you may not grow weary or fainthearted (Heb 12:1–3).

Here is something exceptional: a description of what drives Jesus to do what he does. The one person perfectly ruled by affection (healthy perception and inclination) is motivated by the joy of future reward. We should not be surprised by this. It is not the first time we find this sort of thing in the Bible. I Samuel 17 shows David standing as a type of Christ in slaying Goliath. However, before he fights, David is told three times about the reward he would receive upon his victory. Twice he specifically asks for it to be told to him: "And David said to the men who stood by him, 'What shall be done for the man who kills this Philistine and takes away the reproach from Israel?'...And he turned away from him toward another, and spoke in the same way, and the people answered him again as before" (v. 26, 30).

Jesus acts in hope of future joy. The prize is the redemption of the Church. William Lane argues against this view saying that the author is referring to the joy he left behind, the joy he had with his Father before his incarnation, but Kistemaker, Bruce and Koester all disagree, noting the joy is "set before" him, implying a future joy. The point is that Jesus is moved to action by the things he loves. He is moved to action by the chief of all affections. What is more, the structure of the passage is designed to push us to the same.

The opening word of Hebrews 12, "therefore," both connects and separates the previous chapter. Based on what we have learned about the earlier generations of faithful believers (chapter 11), we need to do something (chapter 12), and it cannot be done alone. Supporting this, William Lane notes a shift in the mood beginning in chapter 12. Chapter 11 was a historical recital, written in the indicative. Chapter 12 is pastoral exhortation, written in the imperative. What is more, while chapter 11 is written in the third person, chapter 12 is in the first and second. The point is that this command of looking to Jesus (v. 2) or considering him (v. 3), is not something that is done alone. Verse 1 is especially emphatic, saying that "even we ourselves"[62] are surrounded by this cloud of witnesses. The author is careful to include himself in the community. Even the cloud of witnesses extends this community. As Lane notes, "In the New Testament, however, a witness is never merely a passive spectator but an active participant who confirms and attests the truth as a confessing witness."[63] The point is that a healthy Christian perseverance requires an active Christian community. To see Jesus well we must see him together. It is important that we not miss this point. Jesus is not among the cloud of witnesses. He is set aside as the founder and the perfector. We do not focus on the cloud, but on him. The cloud, the church, will always disappoint us. It simply can not bear the weight of our expectations, or our needs. But Jesus can, and it is in the company of the church that we see him most clearly.

Like Jesus, it is for the joy of our reward that we persevere. But what is the reward? For Jesus it was us. For us it is him. It is not the

---

[62] Τοιγαροῦν καὶ ἡμεῖς

[63] William L. Lane, *Hebrews 9-13*. Word Biblical Commentary (Dallas, TX: Word Books 1991) 408.

cloud of witnesses (inclusion in a community), or the acceptance of the world (an end to persecutions), but the beauty of Jesus himself that we are called to view. Finally, it is important to note that like Jacob, Moses, David and Isaiah, our desire and privilege is to put our eyes on Jesus.

The Pharisee's Affection

No New Testament writer was more transparent in describing his own desire to see God's glory than Paul. Paul counted all things rubbish compared to knowing God in an affective sense. Even more, he described knowing him as the ordinary Christian experience. This is nowhere more evident than in 2 Corinthians 3.

Paul wrote 2 Corinthians, in part, to confront false teachers who claimed to be apostles and sought to lead the church astray. It appears that their attack became personal as they likely accused Paul of not keeping his word to come visit the church and questioned his apostolic authority. As Philip Hughes notes, Paul responds "with evident distaste for speaking about himself."[64] This quality is seen in chapter 3 where Paul offers the transformation of the Corinthians themselves as evidence of his authority. In other words, his authority is seen in the ministry they have experienced, specifically, an ongoing life-changing encounter with God himself.

> Are we beginning to commend ourselves again? Or do we need, as some do, letters of recommendation to you, or from you? ²You yourselves are our letter of recommendation, written on our hearts, to be known and read by all. ³And you show that you are a letter from Christ delivered by us, written not with ink but with the Spirit

---

[64]Philip Edgcumbe Hughes, *Paul's Second Epistle to the Corinthians*. The New International Commentary on the New Testament (Grand Rapids, MI: Wm. B. Eerdmans Publishing, Co. 1962), xix.

of the living God, not on tablets of stone but on tablets of human hearts (2 Cor 3:1–3).

This is remarkable in itself. False teaching is confronted by an authentic view of God's glory. Or more precisely, false teaching is confronted by the evidence of an authentic view of God's glory.

Paul continues by contrasting the ministry of the old covenant with the new:

> Now if the ministry of death, carved in letters on stone, came with such glory that the Israelites could not gaze at Moses' face because of its glory, which was being brought to an end, [8]will not the ministry of the Spirit have even more glory? [9]For if there was glory in the ministry of condemnation, the ministry of righteousness must far exceed it in glory. [10]Indeed, in this case, what once had glory has come to have no glory at all, because of the glory that surpasses it. [11]For if what was being brought to an end came with glory, much more will what is permanent have glory. [12]Since we have such a hope, we are very bold, [13]not like Moses, who would put a veil over his face so that the Israelites might not gaze at the outcome of what was being brought to an end. [14]But their minds were hardened. For to this day, when they read the old covenant, that same veil remains unlifted, because only through Christ is it taken away. [15]Yes, to this day whenever Moses is read a veil lies over their hearts. [16]But when one turns to the Lord, the veil is removed. [17]Now the Lord is the Spirit, and where the Spirit of the Lord is, there is freedom. [18]And we all, with unveiled face, beholding the glory of the Lord, are being transformed into the same image from one degree of glory to another. For this comes from the Lord who is the Spirit (2 Cor 3:7–18).

The crux for our subject is verse 18. We are changed by beholding him, even as Moses was changed by his time in the tent of meeting.[65] The distinction between Moses and the Corinthians was the external and temporary nature of the glory/change of the old covenant. Verse 3 says that Paul's letter of reference was not written on tablets of stone but rather internally into the very hearts of his readers. However, this does not mean that it did not come with glory. Indeed, it came with enough glory to leave Moses physically changed, but even this change was merely external. Now Paul, the former Pharisee, notes that external behavior, even when it is in compliance with God's law, is not real beauty. Again, this does not mean that there was no glory. Moses' face was certainly changed, but the change itself was merely a hint, a promise of an internal change, a captured authenticity, that is the slow burn of every Christian's desire.

This Exodus viewing of God's beauty was also limited to Moses. Verses 14 and 15 explain that Israel's intellect was veiled and heart hardened. Paul's point was that their hearts, the seat of their emotions, the root of their whole selves remained hardened, or better, their perception inadequate. As Edwards might say, apart from a personal encounter of God's glory our affections cannot be rightly ordered. The result is that Moses's ministry is marked by concealment and Paul's by openness.[66]

Paul describes Moses speaking to Israel with an unveiled face, thus proving the authority of his message. He would then cover his face so that the people would not continue to see the glory, even as it faded. Then, when he would meet with God again Moses would remove the veil (Ex 34:33). Hughes explains that the purpose was so that "the Israelites should not look on the end of that which was tran-

---

[65] Edwards spoke of perception and inclination as the substance of Christian experience. The ability to see ("eyes to see") is the starting place. It is also a gift of his Spirit. Father, open our eyes. Or as the desperate father would say, "I believe; help my unbelief." This prayer is to the Christian what a blasting cap is to the explosion.

[66] Hughes, *Paul's Second Epistle to the Corinthians*, 110.

sient – that they should not see even the impermanent glory without interruption."[67] Thus the veiling of Moses's face was an indictment on the people, the result of their hardened hearts.

Verse 18 however is emphatic: "And we all." Now every believer may see God in a transforming way. It is because of this that Paul could point to the Corinthian's own lives as proof of his apostolic authority as he showed them the transforming beauty of God seen in the effect of the gospel in their lives.[68] Additionally, the result of this beauty is not limited in its duration. "With unveiled face" is a present participle, indicating that the veil remains lifted, it is never hidden.

As such, the ability to discern God's beauty in a way that creates ongoing affective change is portrayed as the ordinary Christian experience. After all, the church in Corinth has never been described as spiritually mature. Instead the ability to see God's beauty makes believers remarkably different from the world, just as it is remarkably true of all believers. As Edwards said:

> For if there be in the saints a kind of perception, which is in its nature perfectly diverse from all that natural men can have, it must consist in their having a certain kind of ideas, or sensations of mind, which are simply diverse from all that can be in the minds of natural men. And that is the same thing as to say, that it consists in the sensations of a new spiritual sense, which the souls of natural men have not... the immediate object of it is the supreme beauty and excellency of the nature of divine things, as they are in themselves. And this is agreeable to the Scripture... "But we all with open face, beholding as in a glass the glory of the Lord, are changed into the same image, from glory to glory, even as by

---

[67] Ibid., 108.

[68] So yes, we fix our eyes on Jesus, but we also fix our eyes on the beauty of the saints—or the great cloud of witnesses.

> the Spirit of the Lord." And it must needs be so, for the Scripture often teaches, that all true religion summarily consists in the love of divine things. And therefore that kind of understanding or knowledge, which is the proper foundation of true religion, must be the knowledge of the loveliness of divine things.[69]

In other words, it is not merely the external, behavioral change that Paul has in mind, but a new sense of the "loveliness" or beauty of divine things. This is the evidence and goal of real faith. But Paul continues to suggest that this reordering of our affections is tantamount to the re-establishment of our humanity. As verse 18 says, as we behold the glory of the Lord we are transformed into the same "image."[70] This is the same word used in the Septuagint to describe our being created in God's image. The point is that our beholding the beauty of God causes us to also reflect that beauty (bear his image) and in a sense to even participate in it. This is the root of the Christian's pursuit of holiness. We might see a person who exhibits a quality of holiness, perhaps a remarkable sense of compassion, and we are then drawn to them and desire to have that same quality in our own lives. By our nature we are drawn to beauty when we see it. But in this case, Paul is describing something that is wholly different. The power of transformation is not our desire, but rather God's glory and the result is an ontological change; we re-gain an aspect of our image-bearing ability. The restoration of the image of God is then our chief ministry. Our authority (or authenticity) is in our reflection of God's holiness, even as Paul's authority was proven by the Corinthians' transformation.

---

[69] *WJE* 2:271.

[70] εἰκόνα

Peter's Affection

It would be difficult to outline the biblical and theological foundations of authentic Christian affection without some consideration of 1 Peter 1:8. Jonathan Edwards sets this verse as the starting place for his *Treatise Concerning Religious Affections* and in a sense the entire book is his exposition.

> Peter, an apostle of Jesus Christ, To those who are elect exiles of the dispersion in Pontus, Galatia, Cappadocia, Asia, and Bithynia, ²according to the foreknowledge of God the Father, in the sanctification of the Spirit, for obedience to Jesus Christ and for sprinkling with his blood: May grace and peace be multiplied to you. ³Blessed be the God and Father of our Lord Jesus Christ! According to his great mercy, he has caused us to be born again to a living hope through the resurrection of Jesus Christ from the dead, ⁴to an inheritance that is imperishable, undefiled, and unfading, kept in heaven for you, ⁵who by God's power are being guarded through faith for a salvation ready to be revealed in the last time. ⁶In this you rejoice, though now for a little while, as was necessary, you have been grieved by various trials, ⁷so that the tested genuineness of your faith—more precious than gold that perishes though it is tested by fire—may be found to result in praise and glory and honor at the revelation of Jesus Christ. ⁸Though you have not seen him, you love him. Though you do not now see him, you believe in him and rejoice with joy that is inexpressible and filled with glory, ⁹obtaining the outcome of your faith, the salvation of your souls.... ¹⁴As obedient children, do not be conformed to the passions of your former ignorance, ¹⁵but as he who called you is holy, you also be holy in all

your conduct, ¹⁶since it is written, "You shall be holy, for I am holy" (1 Pet 1:1–16).

At the start it is difficult to miss the boldness of Peter's tone, especially in comparison to that of Paul in 2 Corinthians. There is no need to establish his authority. He is simply "an apostle." No definite article required. This simple confidence serves to remind his readers that this is the same Peter who lived with Jesus, who saw his transfigured glory, who denied him, and who was restored. And now he is about the business of feeding the sheep. So, when Peter speaks of a "living hope," they are assured that this is not rhetoric. Peter is describing a specific type of hope, one with an animating and independent power that he has experienced. The point is that Peter is not naive regarding the suffering his audience is experiencing. Neither is he fatalistic. Their suffering is real, and so is the power of the gospel.[71]

The result of this power is joy, or as verse 6 says, "in this you rejoice." The first question is to what does "this" refer? In the original the pronoun may be taken as either neutral or masculine and so some have argued that it might best be translated "in whom," thus referring to God the Father (v. 3). This is an attractive translation because it would suggest that our joy is in the person of God rather than any benefit he might offer and so our joy is in the beauty of the person. However, Kistemaker notes that if this were the case the pronoun "whom" would be very far removed from its antecedent in verse 3. A more likely translation is in the neutral, thus "this" would refer to the experience of rebirth and the anticipation of salvation described in verses 3–5.[72] This is also more consistent with what we find in

---

[71] Romans 1:16 speaks of the gospel itself being the power of God. The gospel, which we understand through verbal revelation, is not merely a story, or even an idea. As the means of the display of God's glory it is the agent of change.

[72] Simon J. Kistemaker, *Peter and Jude*. New Testament Commentary (Grand Rapids, MI: Baker Book House, 1987), 46.

verse 9. Regardless, the Christian life is marked with joy, and this joy is based on the gospel promise, on the revelation of God's gracious character. In other words it is a joy based on information leading to a living hope, not mere emotion.

Finally, we come to where Edwards begins: verse 8. Edwards opens by noting the great benefit of such trials in that they first demonstrate the reality of our faith. Indeed, they are called trials because they try the faith of those who profess Christianity. Secondly, such trials make a true faith's "beauty and amiableness remarkably to appear."[73] Finally, trials tend to refine true faith by stripping away things that would otherwise weigh it down. The result is a faith that displays its most genuine beauty.

From here we begin to see Edwards at his best as he notes two "operations," or ways to exercise true religion.[74] The first is that true religion, refined faith, is distinct from ordinary belief in its production of a love for Christ ("though you have not seen him, you love him"). Without seeing with their physical eyes they were led to love Christ, and this, Edwards notes, is a supernatural love. The point is that they saw him spiritually, or in a way different from other experiences, and a wonderment to the world. Second, true religion is distinct in its "inward spiritual joy."[75] This joy is so exceptional, so different than any other kind of joy that there are no human words to describe it ("inexpressible'). From this Edwards concludes the thesis of his work: "Doct. True religion, in great part, consists in holy affections."[76]

Peter goes further in verses 15 and 16 when he connects this joy unspeakable and this love for Christ to holiness. "But as he who called you is holy, you also be holy in all your conduct, since it is written, 'You shall be holy, for I am holy.'" It is worth noting the consistency

---

[73] *WJE* 2:93.

[74] *WJE* 2:94.

[75] *WJE* 2:94.

[76] *WJE* 2:95.

with 2 Corinthians 3 where we see ourselves transformed as renewed image bearers through beholding God's glory. Here we are told to bear his image by displaying his holiness. Holy affections, here seen as joy and love, are a result of a spiritual sense of God's beauty. Elsewhere, Edwards relates his beauty to God's "moral excellency," or holiness. Indeed, Edwards describes this as the spring of all holy affections.[77] So in the end, Peter's exhortation to holiness is an encouragement to simply respond to beauty.

John's Affection

While the primacy of affection is evident throughout scripture, it is difficult to spend any time with the topic without landing on the letter to Ephesus found in Revelation 2:1–7. It is surprising that *Religious Affections* fails to reference these verses in any specific way. Even so, it serves as a good general summary of the topic.

The letters to the seven churches (Revelation 2–3) form a clear literary unit. They also stitch together the introduction and the rest of the book by referring frequently to the language introduced in chapter 1. For example, the lampstand and stars noted in 2:1 refer to the lampstand and stars found in 1:15 and 1:16. Additionally, within this unit are obvious patterns used to address each church, including: a) a charge from the angel to write, b) commendations for good works (except to Laodicea), c) words of encouragement or warning, and d) exhortations to hear and encouragement to those who follow.[78] The point here is simply to note John's careful structure. He is following a pattern; there is nothing accidental about this book. It is appropriate that Ephesus would be addressed first since as a major commercial

---

[77] *WJE* 2:254.

[78] Robert H. Mounce, *The Book of Revelation*. The New International Commentary on the New Testament (Grand Rapids, MI: Wm. B. Eerdmans Publishing, Co., 1977), 84.

center and the junction of several important trade routes it was the most important city in the region.

Beyond the immediate literary structure, Revelation's language and arrangement also demonstrate a conscious connection with the Old Testament as a whole. More than half of the 404 verses in Revelation contain an Old Testament reference, though without any direct quotations. Again, without stringing together quotations, John is following a pattern. He is demonstrating a planned consistency, a progressive revelation. As a result we are not surprised to find a similar consistency in John's earlier work, as the first chapters of John's gospel are written in a careful parallel to the early chapters of Genesis. The themes of life and light are shared, as is the seminal phrase "in the beginning." Equally striking is the gospel's record of the first seven days of Jesus' ministry. So, as in his gospel, John tracks the first book of the Pentateuch, in his revelation he tracks the last.[79] More specifically, as Israel was exhorted to "love the Lord your God with all your heart and with all your soul and with all your might" (Deut 6:5) as the primary direction, the church in Ephesus is commanded to remember the love they had at first. In both cases the command to love, "the chief of the affections," is primary.[80] In addition, it is noteworthy that Ephesus is often cited as a second generation church, being more than forty years beyond its founding. The same might be said of the nation of Israel as they stood before Moses during the preaching of Deuteronomy. At that time, some forty years since their iconic salvation event, rescue from Egypt, God called them to love. Later, Jesus affirms this as the principle command. Now John notes this as the single non-negotiable the church in Ephesus lacked.

> To the angel of the church in Ephesus write: The words of him who holds the seven stars in his right hand, who

[79]Thanks to Charlie Carlberg for a late night and an enticing insight on Revelation as the 5th Gospel.

[80]*WJE* 2:108.

> walks among the seven golden lampstands. ²"I know your works, your toil and your patient endurance, and how you cannot bear with those who are evil, but have tested those who call themselves apostles and are not, and found them to be false.³I know you are enduring patiently and bearing up for my name's sake, and you have not grown weary. ⁴But I have this against you, that you have abandoned the love you had at first. ⁵Remember therefore from where you have fallen; repent, and do the works you did at first. If not, I will come to you and remove your lampstand from its place, unless you repent. ⁶Yet this you have: you hate the works of the Nicolaitans, which I also hate. ⁷He who has an ear, let him hear what the Spirit says to the churches. To the one who conquers I will grant to eat of the tree of life, which is in the paradise of God" (Rev 2:1–7).

In the same way, Deuteronomy stands as a reaffirmation of the covenant before God's people enter the land, extending his kingdom, John's revelation does the same. Now, in the face of persecution, God's church is encouraged to covenant faithfulness, founded in loving affection. As such, the Ephesian Church is told to "remember" (present, imperative) the goodness of God as they had once experienced it. This again is an echo of Deuteronomy where the nation is told fourteen times to "remember" the things the Lord had done among them. In fact while this verb is used fourteen times in Deuteronomy, twelve of which place it prominently in the sentence, it is only used thirteen times in the other four books of the Pentateuch.

Remembering, thinking, reckoning are shown in both Deuteronomy and Revelation to be the fundamental components of love, or rightly ordered affections. Edwards also notes the centrality of the cognitive component. John connects this New Testament affective faith to the very bedrock of the Old Testament Law. This is not a new God, nor is this a new invention. The affective domain has been central to human nature from the very beginning, and viewing God as its greatest desire is central to biblical faith.

Chapter Summary

Each of the characters and texts examined demonstrate the centrality of desiring the person of God, his beauty, his holiness, and his reality, above all other things. Every moment as the church moves forward with God, it is called to a single priority: a lovingly engaged affection. We are not supposed to be nice. We are not supposed to be good people. We are supposed to be in love with something that we find so beautiful that we cannot live without it. From Jacob, Moses, and David's passion to behold the face of God, to Isaiah's affecting view of the same, from Jesus' insistence of the primacy of the heart and love for God, to Paul's promise of the transformative power of God's beauty, from Peter's inexpressible joy, to Revelation's insistence on generational consistency, we find affection, an inclination of desire, at the center of the Christian life. From Moses to the end of time, our covenant is one of authentic love. Simply put, there is no genuine Christian life apart from the affections.

This chapter has sought first to lay a biblical foundation for what comes next. In particular, by looking at individual texts in more detail than is ordinary in Edwards's writings, I hope that his arguments will be more easily understood in the context of their biblical foundation. Second, by describing the affective element of our faith I have sought to engage important topics, and perhaps gain some sympathy, for understanding the concerns of the younger evangelicals.

Chapter 2
Beauty, Sensation, and the Affected Heart

1746 found Jonathan Edwards possessing a crystal sharp mind, filling a prominent pulpit and pastoring a congregation tossed with questions rising from the surrounding revival. His brilliance was in taking seriously what others dismissed, the revival itself, not only on its own terms but as an introduction to the more basic concern of defining the distinctive quality of the Spirit's work. Edwards answered the immediate question regarding the validity of the present revival by answering the larger question: how do we separate genuine spiritual experience from counterfeit; how can we be sure the work being done is God's? His surprising method was exacting empiricism and the result was *A Treatise Concerning Religious Affections*.

Throughout, Edwards stood squarely between two camps. On the one side he faced rising Arminian rationalism, on the other he stood against "new light" emotionalism. In the face of each he argued for a simple and single evidence of genuine Christian experience: gracious affection. We cannot miss the novelty of his approach. "In New England Puritanism, distinguishing between genuine and counterfeit works of the Spirit occurred on three distinct levels: the individual, the ecclesiastical, and the social."[1] In *Religious Affections*, however, Edwards simplifies the argument by considering the individual alone. The result is an exacting treatise designed to weigh individual spiritual experience. Rather than running from the abuses of direct experience, as was common among the "Old Lights," the greater revivalist harnessed empirical sensation and drove it over hard and soft ground alike.

What makes his *Religious Affections* enduringly helpful is, perhaps surprisingly, its polemical quality. The church was not immune to the growing divisions of New England's pre-revolutionary social structure. As George Marsden notes, "These tensions were exacerbated by a gradual transition from the more communal and deferential standards of the Puritan era to the more individualistic tendencies of the eighteenth century, and by the perennial questions of the availability of land for the younger generations."[2] There were political and generational divisions as New England pushed toward a uniquely American social structure. As a result, Edwards was well primed to anticipate and answer objections in a way that would prevent readers from hijacking his work and misrepresenting it for their own purposes. Instead he is so specific in stating what he means, as well as what he does not, that there is little room left for misunderstanding. Clarity is a gift; for Edwards it is nearly a club. Indeed, Edwards chose his language as an illustration of his central premise—religious affection is experienced affection. Put another way, affection is more than ascent. As John E. Smith notes, "The affecting style compels the reader to understand by vicarious participation in what is being described."[3]

---

[1] Ava D. Chamberlain, "Self-Deception as a Theological Problem in Jonathan Edwards's 'Treatise Concerning Religious Affections.'" *Church History* 63 (1994):541–56.

[2] George M. Marsden, *Jonathan Edwards: A Life* (New Haven, CT: Yale University Press, 2003) 125.

[3] *WJE* 2:9.

The result is often difficult reading but when read carefully, *Religious Affections* is equally difficult to misunderstand.

Two Faculties of the Mind

Edwards's arguments tend to begin at the end, end with the middle and throw the beginning in throughout, all the while maintaining a carefully structured argument. The result in *Religious Affections* is a quickly proven conclusion: "Doct. True religion, in great part, consists in holy affections."[4] This is followed by 360 pages of unpacking his terms. Indeed, Edwards chooses his language so carefully that simply understanding his terms enforces his conclusion[5] and so he continues by defining "the affections of the mind" as the "vigorous and sensible exercise of the inclination and will of the soul."[6] He further describes the soul as possessing two faculties: perception and inclination.

It is by perception that we view things. It is by inclination that we approve or reject them. As such, perception is the product of the type of thing we are, allowing or disallowing our ability to see (ontology). Inclination, on the other hand, is a distinctly moral act, to which we are attracted or by which we are repulsed. Of course inclination occurs in various degrees ranging from mild indifference to uncontrollable physical sensation and it is the "more vigorous and sensible" exercises of inclination that Edwards labels "affections."[7] So again, for Edwards, affection is the strong inclination either toward

---

[4]*WJE* 2:95.

[5]This point is among the most helpful insights I can offer to understanding the structure of Edwards's arguments. His language is not difficult because it is dated, but rather because it is exact, and he appears to recognize this, even as this conclusion is quickly followed by: "It may be inquired, what the affections of the mind are. I answer..."(*WJE* 2:96).

[6]*WJE* 2:96.

[7]*WJE* 2:97.

or from a particular thing. Simply put, what we actually choose is what we truly love, and those things are determined by the type of thing we are.[8]

The Primacy of the Heart

In the midst of a church divided between staid orthodoxy and unbridled emotionalism, Edwards presents a tightly reasoned doctrine that avoids the shortcomings of each. By simply defining his terms carefully he argues for the primacy of affection in our faith. True religion "does not consist in weak, dull and lifeless wouldlings, raising us but a little above a state of indifference." Instead, our hearts are to be "vigorously engaged in religion."[9]

It might be argued that Edwards shuts the door to dead orthodoxy by flinging it wide to baseless emotionalism, or put another way, Edwards is simply choosing mysticism over content. But, his emphasis on the transformed will as a consequence of Christian inclination stands in his defense. Affection is proven by willful behavior, and persistent behavior is nothing if not objective.

Roland Delattre furthers this defense noting that for Edwards, the sensation of affection is always the result of viewing the objective beauty of God. "Taken together, beauty and sensibility may be said to be the objective and subjective components of the moral and spiritual life."[10] Or to use the language of *Religious Affections,* inclination is the result of perception. Put another way, we might love a child in theory, but without knowing the child as a person, without knowing

---

[8] If we choose based on the type of thing we are, and we are held accountable for the things we freely choose, then regeneration must precede faith. We must be changed before we freely choose Christ.

[9] *WJE* 2:99.

[10] Roland A. Delattre. *Beauty and Sensibility in the Thought of Jonathan Edwards* (New Haven, CT: Yale University Press. Reprint, Eugene, Oregon: Wipf & Stock, 1968), 3.

that child's name as representing a distinct individual, we are unable to love the child himself. We cannot love what we do not know, and so Christian experience, sensation, will be most affecting when it is based on the most complete study. Put another way, we need to read hard books.

Delattre notes that in *Religious Affections,* Edwards's "primary concern is with sensibility rather than beauty. But even there his objectivism is clear: religious affections are to be tested by their object—'a holy love has a holy object.'"[11] In other words, Edwards does not let his emphasis on sensation run unchecked. Sensation is always the response to objective beauty. We are inclined toward his beauty to the degree that we actually perceive it as objectively real, and so we often pray that God would open blind eyes and unstop deaf ears. In the same way, there is a danger in the church of loving the idea of the gospel without knowing or loving the God of the gospel. Easter is a beautiful idea, and easy to celebrate without dependence on the risen Jesus. The same interaction is found in check-out line devotions promoting faith in faith with little reference to its object. Specificity was at the root of Edwards's language.

Edwards does not respond to the abuses of emotionalism by running from it, but rather by elevating it to the level found in Scripture. Edwards charges into affection more deeply than the most subjective emotionalist, arguing for a unified self where affection, will and religious commitment are indivisible. His advantage was that he could do this simply by describing reality as we experience and Scripture describes it. Put another way, we respond to what we feel so faith without reference to feelings is fractured.

Edwards writes, "We see the world of mankind to be exceedingly busy and active; and the affections of men are the springs of that motion: take away all love and hatred...and the world would be, in a great measure, motionless and dead."[12] He means that nothing

---

[11] Ibid., 126.
[12] *WJE* 2:101.

happens without an affected heart, or what we do is what we love. He finally notes that even the prescribed duties of our Christian lives are designed to have this effect. They are means of grace in that they ordinarily lead to increased affection. Prayer is "but to suitably affect our own hearts with the things we express... And the duty of singing praises to God seems to be appointed wholly to excite and express religious affection." The sacraments, Edwards argues, are the great things of the gospel not simply told but "exhibited to our view... the more to affect us with them." Finally, even God's Word might be effectively taught through "good books of divinity" and provide an appropriate "speculative divinity." Instead, it is preached to impress it on "men's hearts and affections."[13] All of this is quite different than the mere collection of data, or more to the point, data is not rightly collected until it has an affective impact. Perception and inclination are then never separated.

So how do we make ourselves find Jesus more beautiful than the more immediate things? What is Edwards's response to Caroline's honesty? First it is to cry with the desperate father "Lord I believe; help my unbelief." Change the type of thing I am; change what I can seen and how I feel about it. And second it is to join in these prescribed duties. The question is whether we will stand unhealed with Naaman on the shore, or simply step into the river.[14]

Signs of Holy Affection

Having established his conclusion, that true religion consists in holy affections, Edwards defines what are and are not holy affections. He does this through "signs," both positive and negative.

It is important to remember that Edwards offers these signs simply to define what he means by holy or gracious affection. They are not

---

[13] *WJE* 2:115.

[14] 2 Kings 5:1–14.

designed as a test or to provide assurance of salvation. Instead we obtain assurance by one thing, putting to death corruption and increasing in grace. "Assurance is not to be obtained so much by self-examination as by action."[15] Rather, again, he is simply defining what he means when he labels an affection gracious or holy.

First Sign: The New Sense

Scripture speaks of uniquely spiritual qualities such as the spiritual mind,[16] spiritual wisdom,[17] and spiritual blessings.[18] Edwards gathers these together under the idea of a new sense, or spiritual sense of God's beauty. They are "spiritual" because they exist in relation to the Holy Spirit and as an abiding change in the believer's nature. God may choose to impress natural men, as he does with Balaam and Pharaoh, through natural senses but he does so without affecting any sense that is uniquely spiritual.[19]

Instead, for the believer, there is a new indwelling nature. It is not that a portion of our former selves has been intensified, or added to, but rather that a new abiding principle is working under every part.

> This new spiritual sense, and the new dispositions that attend it, are no new faculties, but are new principles of nature.... By principle of nature in this place, I mean that foundation which is laid in nature, either old or new... so this new spiritual sense is not a new faculty of understanding, but it is a new foundation laid in the

---

[15] *WJE* 2:195.

[16] Rom 8:6–7, Jas 3:17.

[17] Col 1:9.

[18] Eph 1:3.

[19] *WJE* 2:206.

nature of the soul for a new kind of exercises of the same faculty of understanding.[20]

With this new nature comes the new, spiritual sense. The believer now experiences reality differently, with a spiritual insight that was not available before. He is now a new creation, something different than before. This cannot be missed if we want to understand Edwards's point. A Christian is a person who goes from being one type of thing to another type of thing, and this change is evidenced in this new sense.

For Edwards, the primary difference between this and a merely natural sense is that this is the result of becoming "partakers of the divine nature" (2 Pet 1:4). God communicates something of his nature. The believer is changed, ontologically, now sharing in something God has given of himself. As this happens "there is a new inward perception or sensation of their minds, entirely different in its nature and kind, from anything that ever their minds were the subjects of before they were sanctified."[21]

In salvation God does not leave the believer lying where he is found, only now holding a bigger stick. The new sense is not an addition, it is a change. And, that change is in the believer's apprehension of God's essential nature, which is specifically holiness. Repentance then becomes an act of hope and confidence that there is something more, something better to come. The believer is different in a way that is as difficult to describe as Edwards is sometimes difficult to read, but then again describing something unknown to our fallen natures is always a thick-tongued exercise.

As such, it is helpful that some of the exercises of loving God are common in loving other things. For example, as a child may desire to please his parents because he loves them, so loving God will make the believer seek God's pleasure. But there is still a fundamental

---

[20] *WJE* 2:206.

[21] *WJE* 2:205.

difference. "That idea which the saint has of the loveliness of God, and the sensation, and the kind of delight he has in that view, which as it were the marrow and quintessence of his love, is peculiar, and entirely different from anything that a natural man has, or can have a notion of."[22] It is tempting to suggest that the difference in sensation is a result of the difference in the object loved. While that, in the end, is true, it is not complete. It misses the point Edwards is making. Instead, Edwards notes the difference in sensation as a result of a change in the one who loves. God underwrites the believer's self with his own essential nature.

> It may be clearly illustrated by this: we will suppose two men; one is born without the sense of tasting, the other has it; the latter loves honey and is greatly delighted in it because he knows the sweet taste of it; the other loves certain sounds and colors (associated with the honey): the love of each has many things that appertain to it, which is common; it causes both to desire and delight in the object beloved, and causes grief when absent, etc.: but yet, that idea or sensation which he who knows the taste of honey, has of its excellency and sweetness, that is the foundation of his love, is entirely different from anything the other has or can have..."[23]

In this, God, as the object of our love, is unique. Art might change the way its viewer thinks or feels (quite a power in itself), but it cannot change what the viewer is able to think or feel. It only suggests, or commends, a thought or sensation that was already resident, though perhaps unexercised. God, on the other hand, changes the nature of the viewer by graciously communicating his own essential nature so that the believer now has access to its range. One is no longer

---

[22] *WJE* 2:208.

[23] *WJE* 2:208–209.

left to love a mere intellectual construction of God, or a theoretical supposition about him, but rather the believer has been made sensible to love God as he truly knows him.

This sense guards against a private or subjective idea of what one loves. Rather than loving an opinion about God, believers love God as he is himself. Rather than loving their participation in the gospel, they love the gospel itself. Believers are more moved by the content of God's word than by the fact that it was made evident to them; they love the things they see of God over the fact that they are permitted to see them. It is a humble faith, so that their affection, whether overtly emotional or stately and quiet, is not a subjective outburst, but an ascent to content gained through this new sense. Their love is certainly personal, but it is never private, because its object is not theirs alone. Comparison and competition have no place in the Christian church.

Second Sign: Lack of Self Interest

Edwards's second sign follows closely on the first. Specifically, it is a view of the "excellent and amiable nature of divine things, as they are in themselves; and not any conceived relation they bear to self or self-interest."[24] Instead of gracious affection, self-love values the lover's experience of the love before the object itself and places the experience in the place of Christ.[25] Instead, "the first foundation of a true love to God is that whereby he is in himself lovely, or worthy to be loved, or the supreme loveliness of his nature."[26] Of course, a believer is only able to experience this second sign if he has already experienced the first.

It is fortunate that many Christian duties are, in themselves, attractive. We are made to live life together, to be other-centered, to

---

[24] *WJE* 2:240.

[25] *WJE* 2:251.

[26] *WJE* 2:242.

proclaim God's glory, and to expand and unify all knowledge under the lordship of Christ. The result is that our fellowship with believers, service to others, public worship, and study of God's word may be independently satisfying. We are made for these things and participation in them is re-humanizing. Even a hardened atheist might enjoy singing Christmas carols with his neighbors, since, at the very moment he is singing that God "makes his blessings flow far as the curse is found," he is experiencing this very fact, albeit as an operation of common grace.

The sad result is that gratitude may rise from self-love, and this gratitude may then be mistaken for gracious affection. Indeed, there may be "the foundation of great affections towards God and Christ, without seeing anything of the beauty and glory of the divine nature."[27] Even so, Edwards does not minimize the benefit, joy and healthy well being associated with salvation. Rather, he insists on these being recognized in their correct order. "Those whose affection to God is founded first on his profitableness to them, their affection begins at the wrong end."[28] The beauty of God is not the offer of Christ, it is the nature of a God who would make such an offer. A view of that nature, and love for it apart from personal benefit, is available through the "new sense" alone.

Our tendency is to replace Christ with our experience of him. Gracious affection loves God himself. Not first that he died for us but that he died for the lost. Not first that he moves toward us, but that he moves toward people. Not first that he has healed us, but that he heals the sick even as he healed the ear of the man who came to carry him to the cross. Our first question is not what sort of beauty would save us but what sort of beauty would save this way?[29]

---

[27] WJE 2:243.

[28] WJE 2:243.

[29] Of his twelve signs, this one seems the most useful as a diagnostic of our spiritual health. To what degree am I moved by the way God saves and to what degree am I moved by the fact that he has saved me?

Third Sign: Love of His Moral Excellency

"A love to divine things for the beauty and sweetness of their moral excellency, is the first beginning and spring of all holy affections."[30] John E. Smith describes this third sign simply as an addition to the second, noting that "the individual may test his affections by this sign if he asks himself the following question: Is my affection arising from a grasp of the beauty of holiness...?"[32] Fair enough, but here is an addition that changes the landscape of Christian aesthetics. While the second sign calls believers to find beauty in God as primary to their happy experience of him, the third directs attention to where, in the person of God, that beauty is found.

Edwards begins by drawing distinctions between God's moral and natural excellency, noting natural excellency as his innate attributes such as honor, strength, etc., and moral as those things done as a moral agent.[33] These are voluntary and seated in his will as a free moral agent, showing the qualities that God himself elects to love.

Drawing primarily on Edwards's private notebook entitled, "The Mind," Louis Mitchell helps define terms explaining that for Edwards, "beauty" displays relations between entities. Those relationships may be rudimentary, such as symmetry of lines or harmony of tones, or more complex, described as "consent," or agreement between entities.[34] It is these more complex relations that Edwards has in mind as his moral, or primary beauty, and these which he finally labels as God's holiness.

---

[30]*WJE* 2:254.

[32]*WJE* 2:30.

[33]The distinction is an interesting cousin to later reformed theologians (Bavnick) communicable and incommunicable attributes. It serves to show an interaction between attributes and excellencies.

[34]Louis J. Mitchell, "The Theological Aesthetics of Jonathan Edwards" *Theology Today* 64 (2007): 36–46.

At this point Delattre is helpful explaining that knowledge of an object's primary beauty involves something that is not required to know its secondary beauty. For example, a listener can enjoy music without understanding harmony.[35] In the same way an unbeliever may know God's secondary beauty without having any particular quality in himself. But to see his primary beauty, to find his holiness beautiful, there must be a change in the viewer.

Even so, Edwards suggests that God's secondary beauty is not rightly seen without a view of his primary beauty because "the true beauty and loveliness of all intelligent beings does primarily and most essentially consist in their moral excellency or holiness."[36] We will look at this in more detail near the end of the chapter, but for now it is important to note that it is the moral beauty that is the true beauty of God's natural perfections. Otherwise, Cruella DeVille would have been resplendent in her Dalmatian coat.

Fourth Sign: The Enlightened Mind

Conrad Cherry noted that while Puritan theologians sought to point at the whole man as subject of faith, "their intention was often markedly frustrated by a faulty psychology that proved inadequate for expressing the unity of the subject."[37] In particular they alternated between the mind and the will as foundational faculties. "Edwards was thus handed by his theological forebears, a clear effort to account for personal unity in the act of faith, but he was also handed a way of accounting for that unity which continually frustrated the effort."[38] Edwards's contribution was in unifying perception and inclination, or mind and will, in the idea of affection.

---

[35] Delattre, *Beauty and Sensibility in the Thought of Jonathan Edwards*, 131.
[36] *WJE* 2:257.
[37] Cherry, *The Theology of Jonathan Edwards, A Reappraisal*, 33.
[38] Ibid., 14.

Simply put, gracious affections arise from information received through the mind. Affections are prompted through information that is either new, or renewed in the believer, or as Paul would put it, our love should abound "more and more, with knowledge and all discernment."[39] Here we see Edwards standing firmly against the anti-intellectualism that is so often associated with revival. He does not allow room for a faith of feeling alone, or a weak-kneed emotionalism. Neither does he allow a faith of mere correct information. Instead, the Spirit is shown to operate upon the whole self through the means of actual content. It is also worth noting that this would be as well received by the ascending enlightenment thinkers of Edwards's day as it is disquieting to the ascending (maybe now declining?) post-moderns of our own. However, for the more careful younger evangelicals in our current churches, those looking for a way between postmodern skepticism and hyper-credulous mysticism, Edwards has cleared a place to stand. He has made a place for Mary Page. More on that later.

At the same time, Edwards avoids a mechanistic view of Scripture, noting that even this cognitive event is only available through an application of the new sense. "There is a distinction to be made between a mere notional understanding, wherein the mind only beholds things in the exercise of a speculative faculty; and the sense of the heart, wherein the mind don't only speculate and behold, but relishes and feels."[40] In this we see an example of Edwards's Locke-esque empiricism interacting with his Calvinistic doctrine of Scripture. Scripture is objectively true but only rightly known in relation to experience.

Perry Miller tends to find Locke peeking around every corner of Edwards's writings and here asserts that Edwards "always exalted experience over reason." He quotes from "A Divine and Supernatural Light" that Edwards "could remember being so young that he thought

---

[39] Phil 1:9.

[40] WJE 2:272.

two objects, one twice as far off as the other, were the same distance away, one above the other; his senses, he reflected, made the same representation of them then as now, and in themselves the senses do not deceive: 'the only difference is in experience.'"[41] But here Edwards stands in contradiction to Miller. Edwards is exalting both reason and experience, noting that religious affection is the result of an increased or renewed reasonable understanding of God's word in concert with the new sense that is available to believers alone.

Of course Edwards's point was not to argue for Locke, or even against him. His point is simply that while an unbeliever may find the Bible in some ways attractive, it is only through the new sense that God's holiness is seen as such. "But spiritual taste of the soul, mightily helps the soul, in its reasonings on the Word of God, and in judging of the true meaning of its rules."[42] In this he is at least adding a new category (spiritual discernment, or inclination) beyond what Locke sought to describe.

Fifth Sign: Effectual Conviction

The fourth sign emphasized the mind's engagement in affection. The fifth emphasizes the mind's certainty. However, it is not a merely speculative or theoretical conviction, but one that is effective unto action. In this sense the fifth sign might be seen as the conclusion of the fourth.

Smith notes that by conviction Edwards has in mind the engagement of the entire self.[43] This certainty, and the believer's willingness to stake everything on it, is presented as a single piece, though it is not given its clearest expression until Edwards's description of the twelfth sign. The point is that this conviction has an effect, or bears fruit. It is

---

[41] Perry Miller, *Jonathan Edwards* (Lincoln, NE: University of Nebraska Press, 1949), 45.

[42] *WJE* 2:285.

[43] *WJE* 2:34.

an "effectual conviction; so that the great, spiritual, mysterious, and invisible things of the gospel have an influence of real and certain things upon them."[44]

Edwards's most original point is that it is beauty that convinces the mind. It does so in two ways. The first is directly: internal and intuitive. It is "a view of this divine glory that convinces the mind of the divinity of these things, as this glory is in itself a direct, clear and all-conquering evidence of it."[45] The idea is simple: there are some things that bear their own evidence. As an illustration, Edwards offers John 1:14.

> [11]He came to his own, and his own people did not receive him. [12]But to all who did receive him, who believed in his name, he gave the right to become children of God. [13]who were born, not of blood nor of the will of the flesh nor of the will of man, but of God. [14]And the Word became flesh and dwelt among us, and we have seen his glory, glory as of the only Son from the Father, full of grace and truth. [15](John bore witness about him, and cried out, "This was he of whom I said, 'He who comes after me ranks before me, because he was before me.'") [16]And from his fullness we have all received, grace upon grace (Jn 1:11–16).

Here, at the center of John's case for Christ's divinity, sandwiched between descriptions of those who did not receive him (11) and those who gave testimony to his truth (15), John offers a remarkably concise summary of the nature of evidence.[46] The objective evidence

---

[44]*WJE* 2:292.

[45]*WJE* 2:298.

[46]Here is where Calvin, VanTil and Gerstner meet in six sentences (five in the Greek). Evidence is objective and real, but always (or only) when viewed by those receiving "grace upon grace."

(dwelling among us), real and convincing in itself, is made effectual through the new sense by which its glory is viewed, tasted and loved. Just as intelligence can sense that Milton is better than Lemony Snicket, the new sense recognizes God's truth as its own evidence.[47]

Secondly, beauty convinces the mind of the truth of the gospel indirectly. While the natural mind is at enmity against God, "when a person has discovered to him the divine excellency of Christian doctrines, this destroys that enmity."[48] Put more simply, the beauty of the gospel (what kind of God would save this way?) allows our objections to quiet. To illustrate, the decisions Ann and I make in disciplining our children do not make sense without seeing the larger beauty of our family, without living with our family, seeing how we also teach our children, read to them, play with them and learn to trust each other. In the same way people who might be offended by the church's position on sexual freedom or the imprecatory Psalms, cannot understand them from outside the fuller family-life context, the indirect evidence. Edwards's larger beauty allows us to trust that the things that are objectionable are family business, and they will make more sense as we live more as family members.

Edwards further notes that grace not only destroys enmity but positively helps reason. The result is that for the believer, external and reasonable arguments serve to strengthen faith, but faith itself is most directly the result of beauty recognized.

Sixth Sign: Evangelical Humility

Edwards writes, "Evangelical humiliation is a sense that a Christian has of his own utter insufficiency, despicableness, and odiousness,

---

[47] Effectual conviction sometimes feels like the one thing we cannot produce, and the one thing we want the most. Edwards is arguing for us to continue further in, further with his word, his church and his worship as the best means to grow that conviction. If truth is it's own evidence then swim in it as much as possible to believe it is as real as water.

[48] *WJE* 2:307.

with an answerable frame of heart."[49] The key here is the term "evangelical." Edwards is speaking of a particular type of humility, or better, a humility that has a particular cause, and in the end has an equally distinct result. The thrust of this point lies in Edwards's distinction between "legal" and "evangelical' humiliation.

Through legal humiliation the mind is well impressed by perception of the natural perfections of God, and through common grace may even be assisted in seeing the response required. But lacking a "new sense" the unbeliever is blind to God's greater beauty and his inclination is left unchanged. In this he is still inclined wholly to himself (see the second sign). He sees no greater beauty than his own comfort, or social standing, or career success, or some other personal benefit, and so in the end his response to God's perfections is a simple calculation toward his greatest benefit. It is the commodification of God. It is the art dealer who calculates the commission before admiring the canvas. It is the college student who enjoys the "fellowship" before loving the people. It is the camp director who fills camp before fostering growth. There may be a willful change, to acquire the art, to confirm to the group, to build the program, but it is in pursuit of a natural affection and has nothing gracious in it. Put another way, "In a legal humiliation, the conscience is convinced, as the consciences of all will be most perfectly at the Day of Judgment: but because there is no spiritual understanding the will is not bowed, nor the inclination altered."[50] The operative term here is "bowed." There is no submission of desire from one beauty to another. Instead, the unbeliever sees service to God, as he understands it, for its strategic value.

It is difficult not to think of Thomas Chalmers' later exposition of 1 John 2:15 in which he notes:

---

[49] *WJE* 2:311.

[50] *WJE* 2:312.

It is thus that the boy ceases, at length, to be the slave of his appetite; but it is because a manlier taste has now brought it into subordination, and that the youth ceases to idolize pleasure; but it is because the idol of wealth has become the stronger and gotten the ascendency, and that even the love of money ceases to have the mastery over the heart of many a thriving citizen; but it is because, drawn into the whirl of city politics, another affection has been wrought into his moral system, and he is now lorded over by the love of power. There is not one of these transformations in which the heart is left without an object. Its desire for one particular object may be conquered; but as to its desire for having some one object or other, this is unconquerable.[51]

This does not mean that legal humiliation serves no holy purpose. Instead, God may use it as a progressing cycle to bring the unbeliever to despair in his ability to affect change, and in this sense it might usefully point the unbeliever to the need for evangelical humiliation. The law may be the means by which God may lead the unbeliever to the gospel. Even so, Edwards notes a legal spirit as being more subtle than is usually recognized and those who mistake one for the other are the most dangerous sorts of believers.[52] Simply put, by definition pride is incapable of naming itself, and so Edwards provides two tests, and while neither is exceptional in itself, his description of each helps open his larger question: how does the new sense continue to underwrite every action of the believer?

The first test for hidden spiritual pride is the unbeliever's tendency to think highly of himself in reference to others. They tend to speak freely of their holiness, and while it is true that every degree of mercy

---

[51] Thomas Chalmers, *The Works of Thomas Chalmers, Complete in One Volume* (A. Towar, Hogan and Thompson Publishing, 1833), 382.

[52] *WJE* 2:318.

is a great thing rightly to be extolled, there is another agent at work here. The key for recognizing the unsaved is not whether they value their experience of holiness as great, but rather that they value it as great in comparison with that of others. The believer, on the other hand, finds his holiness to be a great thing, but meager in reference to that which he desires. He does so for the same reason "a hungry man naturally accounts for that which is set before him, but a little food, a small matter, not worth mentioning, that is nothing in comparison with his appetite."[53]

Here is the leading edge of the issue, the saint, having had something more of God opened to his sight, is convinced of much more than is seen. "As grace increases, the field opens more and more to a distant view, till the soul is swallowed up with the vastness of the object, and the person is astonished to think how much it becomes him to love this God, and this glorious Redeemer."[54] It is this new sense, this new sight, that allows the saint to both despise the thinness of his holiness, and with hope rejoice in the "distant view" of his final participation in the beauty of God's holiness. For the saint, holiness circles around the beauty of God and hopes in him as the "glorious Redeemer." The believer is quietly humble and loudly ambitious for the beauty he now sees.

Edwards's second evidence of hidden spiritual pride is thinking highly of one's humility. Simply put, the proud think more of their humility than the humble because the humble take their measure from what they think their proper height should be.[55] Here again, Edwards is operating from the foundational premise that the believer's new sense, allowing an expanded view of God's beauty in the gospel, serves to fix his eyes on Jesus in a way that bears fruit. So in evangelical humility there is a response to beauty that includes a desire to have more. Legal humility, on the other hand, is a response to power, and

---

[53] *WJE* 2:323.

[54] *WJE* 2:324.

[55] *WJE* 2:332.

seeing God as the solution for the deficit. Each blazes a trail to its true affection.

Seventh Sign: A Changed Nature

This short section, placed in the very middle of Edwards's list, is a simple statement of the root of the matter. For Edwards, as with Paul and Calvin, ontology is found at the center of theology, as faith is more about becoming a new thing than adopting a new behavior or commitment.

"All spiritual discoveries are transforming; and not only make alteration to the present exercise, sensation and frame of the soul; but such power and efficacy have they that they make an alteration in the very nature of the soul."[56] Natural affections may have the power to restrain a man from sin, but restraint is distinct from affection. "A man may be restrained from sin, before he is converted; but when he is converted, he is not only restrained from sin, his very heart and nature is turned from it unto holiness: so that thenceforward he becomes a holy person, and an enemy to sin."[57] To use a somewhat crass illustration, the flies in my barn will always choose to eat a meal that is quite different from what I would eat. They will eat it because they love it, and they love it because they are flies. If, on the other hand, they are changed into men and women, they would then freely love a very different meal. Continuing, both the people and flies are responsible for their choice of meals, they are exercising free will, and it is right that they are accountable for their choices.

Again, the reason for the change is a difference in kinds. The unregenerate is one kind, while the regenerate has become another. Edwards makes allowances for distinctions in "natural temper," noting that "those sins which a man by his natural constitution was most

[56]WJE 2:340.

[57]WJE 2:31.

inclined to before his conversion, he may be most apt to fall into still."[58] But there will still be a change.

The issue here is not the degree of change, but that the change is, again, a change in kind. Something of God is communicated in a nature altering way. Louis Mitchell notes that as such "the saint becomes a partaker of God's beauty:

> [The saints] have spiritual excellence and joy by a kind of participation of God. They are made excellent by a communication of God's excellency: God puts his own beauty, i.e. his beautiful likeness upon their souls.... The saints have both their spiritual excellency and blessedness by the gift of the Holy Spirit, or Spirit of God, and his dwelling in them. They are not only caused by the Holy Ghost, but are in the Holy Ghost as their principle. The Holy Spirit becoming an inhabitant is a vital principle in the soul."[59]

For Edwards, the sense of the heart is not only a vehicle or channel of apprehension and perception, it is "an experience of God."[60] Genuine religious experience is demonstrated in a change in behavior, but it is in fact a change in kind. "But the soul of a saint receives light from the Sun of Righteousness, in such a manner, that its nature is changed, and it becomes properly a luminous thing."[61]

---

[58] *WJE* 2:341.

[59] Edwards, "God Glorified in Man's Dependence," in *Sermons and Discourses, 1730–1733*, ed. Mark Valerie, vol. 17 of *The Works of Jonathan Edwards* (New Haven, CT: Yale University Press, 1999), 2008, as quoted by Mitchell.

[60] Louis J. Mitchell, "The Theological Aesthetics of Jonathan Edwards" *Theology Today* 64 (2007): 36–46.

[61] *WJE* 2:343.

Eighth Sign: A Spirit of Love and Meekness

To this point each of the signs have outlined foundational principles of holy affection. This eighth sign, a spirit of love and meekness is different. It is an exposition of one of the characteristics of Christian character. It is not so much a description of a particular sign, but rather a quality which each sign is "attended with," specifically "the lamb like, dove like spirit and temper of Jesus Christ."[62] While the seventh sign notes that our spirit is changed, here in the eighth we are told how that change appears. It is also noteworthy that immediately following a discussion of allowances for each person's "natural tempers" he begins describing the final result to which each of those tempers will be finally conformed.

Most interesting here is Edwards's description of Christian meekness as a bold weapon in the Christian's warfare. It is likely that this point is informed by his history in Northampton. After two years apprenticing under his father-in-law, Edwards spent the next twenty-two years pastoring this often contentious congregation. And so, he describes Christian fortitude in meekness as withstanding the attacks from outside the church, as well as "suppressing the enemies that are within us; because they are our worst and strongest enemies and have the greatest advantage against us."[63] Again, speaking as a pastor, Edwards exhorts, "True boldness for Christ is universal and overcomes all, and carries 'em above displeasure of friends and foes; so that they will forsake all rather than Christ."[64]

As affections are a response to the object of our faith,[65] love and meekness are the shape of that response. For Edwards this is beyond dispute since they are so clearly seen in the life of Christ.

---

[62]*WJE* 2:344.

[63]*WJE* 2:350.

[64]*WJE* 2:352.

[65]Myron B. Penner, "Jonathan Edwards and Emotional Knowledge of God," *Direction* 30 (2007): 63–75.

Ninth Sign: An Increasingly Softened Heart

It is in the nature of false affections to dull the mind to both sin, present and past, and the unique nature of God's word. In other words, the Bible and awareness of sin become less central to our daily operation, even while the counterfeits confess and convince that they are growing in wisdom and favor with God and man. The result is often an accommodation with a secretly treasured sin. In place of hunger for the word and taste for holiness there is a hunger for comfort and taste for compromise. This all is the result of an application of half the truth. Yes, the saint is saved by grace, but he is also saved unto holiness. The teenager who goes to the water park even though he cannot swim pays the entrance fee for another reason, and the result is danger for both the teenager and the park. In the same way there are some who come to fellowship without any particular affection for Christ, and the result is to do harm to both the church and themselves. "They trust in Christ to preserve 'em the quiet enjoyment of their sins, and to be their shield to defend 'em from God's displeasure; while they come close to him, even to his bosom, the place of his children, to fight against him, with mortal weapons, hid under their skirts."[66] There are orphans among the family, and these orphans are always traitors.

Gracious affections are different. The more that is seen of God's beauty the more it is desired so these affections tend to soften the heart, "making it tender, and to fill it with dread of sin, or whatever might displease and offend God."[67] They want to learn to swim, and to become very good at it. Again, this is the result of a fuller view of our salvation, and in particular the holiness for which we are saved. So "the banishing of a servile fear, by a holy assurance, is attended with an increased reverential fear. The diminishing of the fear of the fruits of God's displeasure in future punishment is attended with a

---

[66] *WJE* 2:359.

[67] *WJE* 2:360.

proportional increase of fear in his displeasure itself: the diminishing of the fear of hell, with an increase of the fear of sin.[68] "Like David's heart, that smote him, when he cut off Saul's skirt. The heart of a true penitent is like a burnt child, that dreads the fire."[69]

Tenth Sign: Symmetry of Virtues

It is surprising that there is not more written on Edwards's tenth sign. It is here that his philosophy becomes theology and then is made practical. Specifically, primary and secondary beauty are seen on a single screen, and that screen is best polished as a mirror.

Edwards begins with the relieving qualification that no symmetry of virtues can be perfect. We lack perfect instruction and battle natural "tempers," so our sanctification is sadly variegated. Even so, the Spirit's work within the believer is evident. "There is, in no wise, that monstrous disproportion in gracious affections, and the various parts of true religion in saints, that is commonly to be observed in the false religion and counterfeit graces of hypocrites."[70] Instead, the whole image of Christ is impressed on the believer as the Spirit is truly communicated, as he is truly in reality, not merely in the ways he is most fitting to the believer's disposition. In other words, the Spirit is not a magic endowment to empower the believer's pre-disposed strengths, but rather he gives a new nature infecting every faculty with a new inclination. There is a putting off the old man as a whole, not merely a selection of its qualities, and putting on a new man. Again, this may be halting, and at times inconsistent, but the process moves forward as a piece.

It is worth noting this in regards to Galatians 5, where Paul speaks of the unity of the Spirit's work in the believer's life.

---

[68] *WJE* 2:365.

[69] *WJE* 2:364.

[70] *WJE* 2:365.

> But the fruit of the Spirit is love, joy, peace, patience, kindness, goodness, faithfulness, [23]gentleness, self-control; against such things there is no law. [24]And those who belong to Christ Jesus have crucified the flesh with its passions and desires.

The obvious first point is that both "fruit" and "Spirit"[71] are singular. There is one Spirit and his single work is evidenced in a constellation of qualities, but these qualities are taken as a whole. To gain entrance to Ft. Bragg an officer must have both a uniform and military ID. To have the uniform without the ID does not constitute proof of his status. In the same way, to have joy without self-control is not a uniquely Christian quality, and so Edwards joins Paul in insisting on symmetry of virtues. Regeneration is a whole self being transformed in its whole self. "There is no grace in Christ, but that there is its image in believers to answer it... there is feature for feature, and member for member."[72]

The result is that the whole image of Christ is impressed upon his children, not a portion. Every element of the fallen nature is subject to any true work of the Spirit, a prospect that is celebrated by the believer as it is terrifying to the unbeliever. Beauty wants to be owned, not in the sense of being controlled, but rather resident. So as believers sing and talk about the beauty of Christ they, by nature, join his holy jealousy on their behalf, wanting to be perfect as he is perfect.

The result is integrity, and sensibility arising from a new affection as its key. By locating the mind, will and emotion under the single idea of affection (through perception and inclination) Edwards establishes an integrated self. Delattre ties this up nicely saying that

> where the understanding is sensible, where the mind does not only 'speculate and behold, but relishes and feels' [RA

---

[71]καρπὸς, Πνεύματός.

[72]WJE 2:365.

272], approves or disapproves, likes or dislikes, loves or hates, consents or dissents, then there is in Edwards' view such an integrity in the self that no clear distinction can be made 'between the two faculties of understanding and will acting distinctly and separately' [RA 272].[73]

The distinction between natural affections and gracious (that which is the result of God graciously communicating something of his nature to the believer) is sometimes subtle. Unbelievers may at times demonstrate seemingly gracious affections toward certain things but also "partiality and disproportion" with regard to different objects. For example, believers are called to love the church, but often (always?) find some members less lovely. Of course there is a degree to which believers may also react to the halting nature of personal holiness in the one loved. But, there is also a sense in which believers will recognize God's grace to them and desire to offer the same to their brothers. It is in the nature of gracious affection for a growth in our strength to also have a corresponding growth in our humility, or an increased love for the most attractive church member to have a corresponding love for the least attractive.

Additionally, natural affection is seen as distinct from that which is gracious in the way believers demonstrate their love for the same person. Natural affection may be gracious in meeting physical needs, or in meeting spiritual needs, but gracious affection will move toward each. Likewise, natural affection may be gracious in pursuing truth, or in pursuing justice, but gracious affection will move toward each. Natural affections appear as the result of what one holds by his own strength as afforded by common grace. In this natural affection is a love for our own natural excess rather than a love for what God has graciously provided.

Again, this symmetry is imperfectly evident in the lives of believers, but still real, and according to Edwards, it is always evident. "The

---

[73] Delattre, *Beauty and Sensibility in the Thought of Jonathan Edwards*, 7.

body of one that is born a perfect child, may fail of exact proportion through distemper, and the weakness and wounds of some of its members; yet the disproportion is in no measure like that of those that are born monsters."[74] Because for the believer there is also real hope of an inevitable gravitational pull to beauty.

Consider the beauty of Jesus, always treating each person exactly as needed. He met one of Lazarus's sisters with confrontation, and the other with tears. He attacked the money changers and invited the tax collector. He commanded the waves, confronted the disciples and comforted the thief. He always chose the right tact. Now consider your last three disagreements and you will become very hungry for this beauty, this symmetry of virtues to be real in your own life. Here is the beauty of our God. Here is the beauty of his holiness being communicated to his church. Here is our promised trajectory.

Eleventh Sign: Increasing Desire

Edwards is a strange mix in that he makes different people uncomfortable for opposite reasons. Those who have not read him are often uncomfortable with his reputation as a strict, Calvinistic Puritan. They imagine a cold, unbending, humorless preacher. They suppose raised voices, stern expressions, and rigid orthodoxy. Those who have read him only slightly often have an opposing fear. They read of his emphasis on affection and religious experience and, without fully understanding his terms, prepare a stance against a less bridled, mystic, spiritual inwardness. Edwards subtly and biblically avoids both errors. Even so it must be noted that his eleventh sign is among his most subjective.

Edwards argues that it is a sign of true and gracious (given by God as a matter of grace) affection that the more it is present the more the appetite for God is increased. Moreover, gracious affection is humble in its want of more, as opposed to false affection that is "self-content

---

[74]*WJE* 2:365.

and self satisfied."[75] Conversely, the more a believer hates sin "the more he desires to hate it, and laments that he has so much remaining love to it."[76]

Edwards gives a single reason why these things are the case, and from this a second reason might also be implied. His reason is that it is the result of an actual change in the believer as spiritual health shows its fruit. Edwards illustrates simply, "'Tis the nature of a newborn babe, to thirst after the mother's breast; who has the sharpest appetite, when best in health."[77] To carry the metaphor further, believers have a greater hunger for Christ as their taste is refined, and here the refining is a clearer view of their need for grace. As such "I believe; help my unbelief!" is cried most loudly by those most faithful. A second reason for this increasing attraction is the nature of the attracting object. The natural man's attraction is to his own benefit. The believer's is to the beauty of God. The first is finite, and will finally be sated. The second is infinite and can not be exhausted, so that the children's call advancing into Aslan's country of "further up and further in" continues on and on for the believer. Or put another way, the gravitational pull of a planet is greater as its moon is drawn closer.

Edwards fleshes out his premise by answering the anticipated objection that a mandatory increasing desire would not leave room for satisfaction in the gospel. Instead he notes first that the things of the gospel are satisfying in that they are perfectly appointed to the nature of man. In other words, it is in our nature to be satisfied by an increasing hunger. There is an "expectation of the appetite" that is bound to the nature of the object desired.[78] The implication is that our experience of a boundless God can only be answered by a boundless hunger. Any other reaction would not satisfy because it

---

[75] WJE 2:39.

[76] WJE 2:377.

[77] WJE 2:377.

[78] WJE 2:379.

would be self-evidently false. Thirdly, Edwards notes that satisfaction, as it has been described, is permanent. Worldly affections might be glutted, or sated because they correspond to a finite object and so can, and must, be exhausted. Finally, Edwards notes that the believer's satisfaction can rest in the fact that our God will never be exhausted. "There is enough room here for the soul to extend itself; here is an infinite ocean of it."[79] Here is the thing we are made for.

Edwards's genius here is seen in placing the subjectivity of our desire and satisfaction on the objectivity of the nature of God himself. So here, where Edwards might otherwise be accused of severe mysticism, he stands on severe, even infinite, objectivity. This is the ground he has cleared for our more modern evangelicals.

On a more practical level we note that in the midst of the Great Awakening, when so many would seek God for a season only, and others for the whole of their lives, Edwards notes a continuing and deepening hunger for the things of God as evidence of having him in the first place. There can be no relying on past experiences except that they cheer us on toward those that are in addition and increased.

Twelfth Sign: Christian Practice

The symmetry of Edwards's argument is seen in this last sign of gracious affection. He begins with the most subjective, and perhaps most esoteric of the signs, the new sense, and now ends with the most objective, most concrete. While the balance offers bipolar bookends, the greater detail devoted to this final sign shows where Edwards felt the greatest need for the church lay. His immediate context in particular swirled with new questions regarding eligibility for church membership and participation in the sacraments. The length of this section also hints that there is more to this point than at first meets the eye.

---

[79] *WJE* 2:379.

For Edwards, gracious affections are most clearly seen, and have "their exercise and fruit in Christian practice."[80] This is first evidenced in consistent behavior, or as Edwards says, the fact that believers are to be "universally obedient."[81] As an example, Edwards cites Naaman, who appeared to be greatly affected with gratitude to God for his healing, but still desired to be excused from one thing. "It is necessary that men should part with their dearest iniquities which are as their right hand and right eyes..."[82] The point is simple, and not unrelated to his tenth sign, the symmetry of virtues. Inclination toward the beauty of God is unto the actual God, not a composite of preferred attributes. The internal dynamics of the heart, rooted in a new sense (first sign), a view of God's moral excellency (third sign), and an enlightened mind (fourth sign), will lack self interest (second sign) and invest fully in allegiance to God as he is in reality and the result will be a desire to conformity throughout.

Second, gracious affection will be evidenced in a serious diligence. The pursuit of holiness and the ambition to advance the kingdom is not a light thing in the life of the believer. As David sought one thing so the believer will have a primacy of purpose, and this inclination will finally result in diligent Christian service.

Finally, true Christian faith is evidenced in perseverance through the trials and temptations that will compete for his ultimate allegiance. In this Edwards acknowledges that any long-lived believer will encounter difficult circumstances and, at times, and for a period, experience some degree of backsliding, "but they can never fall away so, as to grow weary of religion, and the service of God, and habitually to dislike it and neglect it."[83]

---

[80] WJE 2:383.

[81] WJE 2:384.

[82] WJE 2::386.

[83] WJE 2:390.

From here Edwards continues, claiming ground that is seldom traveled. The question is, as noted by John Smith, how to reconcile the apparent contradiction between the primacy of the heart and the requirement to conform to the law.[84] Christian practice is to Edwards the chief of all evidences of gracious affections because it is objective and observable. It is an accurate test because behavior that is consistent, diligent, and persevering is the result of an internal, ontological reality: "They (holy behaviors) flow from a divine communication (real giving) of God, a participation in the divine nature."[85] False affections do not reach the foundation, they are not deep enough to rule all of our actions.

Instead, false affections are based on self-interest. As such they are active only to the degree to which they serve their purpose. For example, a believer may deceive himself and others, because he finds comfort in the church community, or a child at summer camp may confess Christ because she desires the qualities she sees in her counselors or other believing campers. But, this is a desire for the results of faith rather than affection for the God of faith. Instead, for the believer "seeing holiness is the main thing that excites, draws and governs all gracious affections... that which men love they desire to have and to be united to, and possessed of. That beauty which men delight in, they desire to be adorned with."[86] Here is the Christian aesthetic. Believers desire holiness simply because they find it beautiful. This change is enduring because it is driven by a change in nature. We are always changed by the thing we desire, and we desire what we find beautiful.

Edwards reaches a simple conclusion in a remarkable way. He shows observable Christian practice is the chief sign of true faith by giving an objective footing to the internal nature of faith. As Conrad Cherry has said, "One had best leave the mantle of 'mysticism' for

[84] *WJE* 2:41.
[85] *WJE* 2:392.
[86] *WJE* 2:394.

another wearer than Edwards, for it fits him loosely at best...for in Edwards 'spiritual inwardness' never replaces but complements the visible means of grace and the outward orientation of faith."[87] Cherry's point is that Edwards establishes the reality of this inwardness on the foundation of observable evidence, which is as objective as the nature of God himself.

The whole of his point is put most succinctly by John Smith who says,

> This is the crux of the matter; taking conduct as a sign is a matter not merely of discovering whether it conforms to rules but of learning how and in what way it reveals the heart. Practice, then, cannot be viewed merely as a doing or abstaining, for we must discover in a man's conduct the true affections of his heart.[88]

The Cause of Changed Affections

It is difficult to wade into *Religious Affections* without being struck with two competing ideas. First, there is hope that such a remarkable heart for loving God is not only available, but that it is to be ordinary to Christian experience. The very moment of having this idea is itself an experience of what it describes, and we are encouraged noting that "Hope in the Lord is also frequently mentioned as the character of the saints."[89] This hope is not wishful thinking, it is firm confidence in the final destination of our trajectory. With each paragraph we are more neatly cornered into agreeing that the reality behind the words is beautiful and affecting; our faith is more beautiful than we dared believe before. It is more than a construction of system upon systems,

---

[87] Cherry, *The Theology of Jonathan Edwards, A Reappraisal*, 88.

[88] *WJE* 2:41.

[89] *WJE* 2:103.

logic upon logic, belief upon beliefs. It is systems based on seeing, logic based on loving and believing based on beholding. The result is more than a mere belief in the gospel; it is a sense of its beauty. It is exactly what the enlightenment stole from the church.

The second idea is concern. With every line of exacting logic we are more convinced of how little of this is true of us. As Edwards says, this shows

> what great cause we have to be ashamed and confounded before God, that we are no more affected with the great things of religion.... In things which concern men's worldly interest, their outward delights, their honor and reputation, and their natural relations, they have their desires eager, their appetites vehement, their love warm and affectionate.[90]

The hope here is that Edwards begins in the first person plural, including all believers, and specifically himself, in this wounded fellowship. The concern is that he ends with the third person plural, leaving the question of whether the reader is "we" or "they." But even here Edwards is exceedingly practical, noting that the reason for the distance between our hope and fear is that we are "often mixed" and so "the degree of religion is rather to be judged by the fixedness and strength of the habit that is exercised in affection, whereby holy affection is habitual, than by the degree of present exercise."[91] In other words our hearts are better measured by their trajectory than their location.

So the question is this: what is the means by which this trajectory is changed, or what is the means by which God affects change in the affections? In more traditionally Puritan language, according to Edwards, what are the means of grace in relation to our affections?

[90] WJE 2:122.

[91] WJE 2:118.

In his "Personal Narrative" Edwards outlines a brief history of his own growth in affection. It is a remarkably practical document because it is written as a simple biography rather than a theological treatise. His point is to describe his experience, not justify it, but by placing this alongside *Religious Affections* we have both a description and an illustration. In his narrative, Edwards describes personal seasons of spiritual activity, beginning as a child (when at age eight he had a sort of fort in the woods where he and other boys would meet to pray), reviving in college, and finally becoming more consistent as a young man. Throughout there were "great and violent inward struggles" which were finally put to rest with an increased love for God's sovereignty. Even so, Edwards confessed that he "never could give an account, how, or by what means, I was thus convinced, not in the least imagining at the time, nor a long time after, that there was any extraordinary influence of God's Spirit in it; but only that now I saw further." Instead, Edwards seems to describe seasons of false affections, finally leading to a life of gracious affection. In his narrative, Edwards refuses to give a formula for changed affections. Instead he gives a description of its results. The reason is that he saw gracious affection to be the result of God's sovereign Spirit, not something achieved by works. But, in *Religious Affections* Edwards goes a step beyond his described experience, outlining the effectiveness of several of the traditional means of grace (prayer, singing praises, sacraments and the word preached), as referenced earlier.[92] He also gives a more detailed description of suffering and its specific relation to affection.

Suffering

Edwards is difficult to read in the same way that faith is difficult to describe. Instead of building premise upon premise with an inevitable final conclusion, he begins describing the interior life of the believer,

[92] *WJE* 2:58.

and then circles back showing its logical consistency and biblical requirement. In the same way faith, which is often adopted before it is carefully proven (be honest, why did you first believe?), is foreign to the skeptic. We simply do not have the language to describe it, or the faculty to understand it, until after we have experienced it.

And so, Edwards begins *Religious Affections* quoting 1 Peter 1:8: "Though you have not seen him, you love him. Though you do not now see him, you believe in him and rejoice with joy that is inexpressible and filled with glory." He continues, "In these words, the Apostle represents the state of the minds of the Christians he wrote to."[93] He begins then, with the interior idea, or state of mind, that most directly leads to true faith, one wrought by suffering and trials of faith. "They, above all other things, have a tendency to distinguish between true religion and false, and to cause the difference between them to evidently appear." In this Edwards is not describing suffering as a means of grace, but rather a means by which faith is made evident. That evidence then becomes a means of grace. Given his immediate need of distinguishing true believers from false in the rush of revival, it is not surprising that Edwards would start here.

Next, Edwards notes that trials do more than demonstrate the presence of saving grace; they display its beauty. This is not the same as saying that trials show the beauty of Christ, rather they do show the beauty of his work, by which we know him. In both of these descriptions Edwards is showing trials and suffering as a clarifying glass through which the presence and beauty of faith are seen clearly. Again, at this point Edwards has not gone so far as to say that trials purify our faith. That point is still to come, but for now he is making the more original observation that trials tend to showcase the beauty of real faith.

His third point is that trials tend to "purify and increase" true faith. Seeing the reality and beauty of faith, even, or perhaps especially, the reality and beauty of faith in one's own life, causes it to increase. They

---

[93] *WJE* 2:93.

"deliver it from those mixtures that which is false, which encumber and impede it; and nothing may be left but that which is true."[94] Edwards's brilliance is not this conclusion, but the method by which it is reached. Faith is refined and increased by its beauty being demonstrated, by its idea being imprinted on the senses as reality. It is then no surprise that throughout Scripture "glory" (δόξα) occurs most often with verbs of appearing (e.g. Rom 8:18: For I consider that the sufferings of this present time are not worth comparing with the glory that is to be revealed to us). Even the idea of glory is related to brightness, radiance and splendor, all visual events. The language used here is to impart a sense, or impress an idea upon our senses. The beauty of faith is shown as connected to its objective reality. As it is shown to be real, proven by evidence, it is shown to be beautiful. Trials "tend to cause the amiableness of true religion to appear to the best advantage, as was before observed; and not only so, but they tend to increase its beauty, by establishing and confirming it, and making it more lively and vigorous."[95] So trials reveal the nature and beauty of true faith, which in turn causes its increase as the believer is more effectively inclined toward the more evident beauty.

The Christian practice of endurance under trials is not merely evidence of faith. It is evidence affording a better view, which then necessarily produces a better faith. The Christian life carries its own means of increasing momentum. As Jesus describes, "to everyone who has will more be given, and he will have an abundance. But from the one who has not, even what he has will be taken away" (Mt 25:29). Those who are able to perceive, because of the type of thing they are (redeemed humanity, or a person in the barn, not a fly in the barn), are also more effectively inclined toward the beauty revealed. They eat good food and so are healthy enough to eat more good food. False faith, promoted by some false-god, lacks this circular power. For a time it may move a person in the same direction as holiness, but this

---

[94] *WJE* 2:93.

[95] *WJE* 2:93–94.

lacks the power to move her heart, or change her affection. Rather than a new sense of the beauty of Christ, there is the familiar sense of the benefit to the individual. But when this benefit (the enjoyment of the church's company, a merely ecstatic worship experience, the admiration of peers, etc.) is brought under the saddle of suffering it is discovered dead in a hole.

Two Operations of Faith

If showing faith to be present demonstrates its beauty, and showing its beauty makes it desirable, then, Edwards continues, faith's two operations, the things it ordinarily does, contribute to our "new sense" of God's excellency. Referring again to 1 Peter 1:8, Edwards describes the first of these as the believer's increasing love to Christ. This increasing love is evidence of God's beautiful and supernatural work. Writing to second generation believers, Peter says that while they had not seen Christ with their eyes, they had nonetheless seen him spiritually. That this object of sense caused them to reject the world which they saw physically, choosing trials and suffering instead, stood as evidence of the greater beauty apprehended by the new sense. What appears to the world as repulsing foolishness appears to the church as attracting beauty. This sort of love for Christ is the first operation of faith.

Edwards's second operation of faith, joy in Christ, stands also as testimony to the superior nature of this real faith over false. It is not just that joy arises as evidence of things not seen, but rather that the joy is so different from ordinary experience that it is described as "inexpressible." Its nature cannot be expressed because it is uniquely different from other shared experience; it is new. Therefore it is demonstrated as supernatural in that it fills "minds with the light of God's glory, and made 'em themselves to shine with some communication of that glory."[96] The point is not simply that the believer is filled

[96] WJE 2:95.

with joy, but that he is filled with a kind of joy, namely a joy that is inexpressible, or qualitatively different from ordinary joy. Here is the point: because grace has been "communicated" in a way that changes the believer, he must always demonstrate something of that grace, and Peter describes this demonstration as evidenced by indescribable joy. This joy is uniquely Christian and in its relation to the new sense.

So while this joy is distinct and so cannot be well described (inexpressible),[97] this does not mean that there is nothing that can be said of it. Indeed, Peter describes it as "full of glory."[98] This uniquely Christian, indescribable joy is most closely associated with glory, or the revelation of God's beauty. "In rejoicing with this joy, their minds were filled, as it were, with a glorious brightness, and their natures exalted and perfected... it filled their minds with the light of God's glory, and made 'em themselves to shine with some communication of that glory."[99]

The communication in mind here is not communication from the believer to the world, but rather communication of God's glory to the believer. And it is important to realize that Edwards is using "communication" as an actual giving rather than a mere description. Here we see this giving evidenced in a unique, inexpressible joy, rising from faith, which is demonstrated as both beautiful and exceptional by its growth during suffering.

---

[97] It is disappointing that Edwards did not spend more time describing this word in light of his emerging empiricism, and the growing conversation regarding the ability of language to represent reality. As he famously noted in other places, the difference between the description of an event and its reality is like the difference between being told honey is sweet and tasting it for oneself. It is in this sense that Christian joy is inexpressible, as is the distinction between gracious affection and false.

[98] δεδοξασμένη is a passive participle denoting praise, glory and splendor. This is a nearly perfect use of a participle, even defining the part of speech: having properties of both a verb and an adjective. The verbal sense of revealing is the reason for its use as an adjective, denoting glory and splendor.

[99] WJE 2:95.

Sensation and Beauty

For Edwards the problem with the Old Lights was the same as with the New. For both the staid, traditional, New England insider and the ecstatic, progressive, individualistic outsider, the argument is about psychology and metaphysics more than theology or logic. The problem for Edwards is communication rather than information. Here Edwards launches out, casting true religion beyond intellectual ascent. Not that faith is less than intellectual agreement, but it is certainly more, and that more is love. Love is the final expression of inclination, and inclination is a result of our apprehension and movement toward an object's inherent beauty. While affirming the classical Puritan doctrine of our passive reception of grace, Edwards develops the idea further than had been done before, adding that apprehension happens as the beauty of God's truth is impressed upon our minds. That impression is always through our senses. Rather than believing on the basis of concepts, the church loves on the basis of inclination, resulting from the sensation of beauty. Our reception of grace is to have been given sight, or the new sense. As Perry Miller has noted, "If he perceives in a cold, dull lifeless frame, the coldness is not the inert object, but his own. 'He that is spiritually enlightened truly apprehends and sees it, or has a sense of it.' To see is to have a sense; to have a sense is to have an inclination; and as a man inclines, he wills."[100] This is all simply to say again that our love for Christ is not our agreeing that he is beautiful, but experiencing that beauty as a controlling idea.

The Christian Sermon

As a result the Christian sermon serves a different purpose than it appears to in some evangelical churches. Rather than demonstrating

---

[100] Miller, *Jonathan Edwards*, 65.

the logic of true statements it is now designed to impress on the mind, through the senses, the nature of the truth found in the text. The purpose is more than just discriminating correct information; it is a means by which to communicate reality.[101] "Hence Edwards's pulpit oratory was a consuming effort to make sounds become objects, to control and discipline his utterance so that words would immediately be registered on the senses not as noises but as ideas."[102] If beauty is perceived through the senses then preaching must be sensational, meaning it must convey the weight, or sense, of the subject. In this light his famous Enfield sermon, "Sinners in the Hands of an Angry God," is not an exception to his otherwise philosophical bent, but rather an example of its best application. The language and images were designed to give a sense of the idea, or reality of his text. There was no attempt to drum up emotional response or produce a hysterical reaction. Instead, his sermon uses the correct words which best stand for the substance of the ideas beneath them, and so his images, most notably that of the condemned spider, are more than evocative metaphors. They are designed to impress the idea of the text upon the senses. The irony is that the sermon most often offered as an example of emotional pandering is anything but. It is instead a careful meeting of philosophy, anthropology and theology as introduced by the biblical text itself.

Consent to Being

In *Religious Affections,* Edwards's primary concern is with sensation, apprehension and communication of beauty. But he must define the nature of that beauty as an element in itself. For Edwards, beauty is

---

[101]Again, to "communicate" is a giving of the thing itself rather than mere information about the thing. In this sense all true communication is sensual and all true preaching is spiritual. It is dependent on the Spirit's work.

[102]Miller, *Jonathan Edwards,* 158.

more than an attribute of God. It is his defining essence. "God is God, and distinguished from all other beings, and exalted above 'em by his divine beauty."[103] Sensation of that beauty is the distinguishing mark of the believer. As such Edwards's description of God's beauty is his most important theological/philosophical contribution. While others, most notably Augustine, Aquinas and Barth, have made some contribution here, Edwards is alone in housing all of God's perfections under the overarching structure of his beauty. He is the theologian of aesthetics, and the preacher of sensation. As Ronald Delattre notes,

> The greater stress upon immediate experience was already a major contribution of Puritanism before Edwards' time; in this respect he was less of a pioneer and more of a perfector. But in the manner in which he places beauty at the center of his conception of God he was indeed a pioneer, moving into terrain scouted but never systematically settled.[104]

In categorizing God most essentially as beautiful Edwards describes both his moral and natural perfections, or philosophically, his secondary and primary beauty. Natural perfections refer to his greatness, and moral perfections to his holiness; secondary beauty refers to objects and their balance and proportion to one another, and primary beauty refers to objects and their ideas in their moral relation, or inclination, to the other. As Delattre explains:

> Primary beauty, variously referred to as true, highest, moral, spiritual, divine, or original beauty, consists in one kind of consent or agreement: the cordial or heartfelt consent of being to being. It is essential to primary beauty that the will, disposition, or affection of the heart be involved in the consent. Secondary beauty, inferior to

---

[103] *WJE* 2:298.

[104] Delattre, *Beauty and Sensibility in the Thought of Jonathan Edwards,* 121.

the former and otherwise referred to as natural beauty, consists in a very different sort of agreement or consent... that is "a mutual consent and agreement of different things, in form, manner, quantity, and visible end or design; called by the various names of regularity, order, uniformity, symmetry, proportion, harmony," and "uniformity in the midst of variety" TV 28.[105]

In other words, the difference between God's natural perfections, or secondary beauty, and God's moral perfections, or primary beauty, is the exercise of the will. A face may be pleasing because of its symmetry, a garden because of its balance of elements, the front of a home because of the scale of its entry in relation to its front wall, or a piece of music because of its recurring pattern and final resolve. Each of these is beautiful because of their relation or "consent" to other elements. On the other hand, moral perfection, or primary beauty, is a balance, or proportionality, resulting from an act of will. Love and choice are then the highest forms of beauty.

By defining terms Edwards enforces a remarkable conclusion: beauty is objective, and our apprehension of it is observable. In particular, primary beauty is objective in its relation to something outside of itself. Delattre elaborates that primary beauty "is defined by reference to the object of consent. If it is the consent of minds toward minds, it is love, and if it is minds towards things, it is choice."[106] Beauty is limited by the nature of the object, and so final, objective beauty can only be found in God.[107] Remembering that inclination is that by which we choose action, and perception is the predecessor to inclination, we can work backwards to the conclusion of *Religious*

---

[105] Ibid., 17.

[106] Ibid., 21.

[107] So here is why we will be satisfied by nothing less than the Trinity. Even the idea of God, or a perfectly inclusive community will fall flat. We will remain hungry until there is an actual communication of God himself.

Affections: beauty cannot be truly known without being enjoyed, or "True religion, in great part, consists in holy affections."[108]

The point is that to have a sense, or an affecting view, of God's holiness/beauty, is evidence of an ontological change in the believer. So, for the believer, affection is objective. It is also required.

> By this sight of the moral beauty of divine things, is seen the beauty of the way of salvation by Christ.... By this is seen the excellency of the Word of God.... By this is seen the true foundation of our duty.... And by this is seen the true evil of our sin.... By this men understand the true glory of heaven.... By this is seen the amiableness and happiness of both saints and angels.... He that sees the beauty of holiness, or true moral good, sees the greatest and most important thing in the world.... Unless this is seen, nothing is seen.[109]

And so the exhortation in Hebrews to "fix our eyes on Jesus, the author and perfector of our faith" gains weight (12:2a, NIV). Fixing our eyes on Jesus as the author of our faith proves the previous quotation's first and last sentences. Fixing our eyes on him as the perfector of our faith proves everything between. And so here we find both the simplicity and the difficulty of our faith. We have a single thing to do: join Moses and Jacob in their desire to gaze on beauty. But that single thing is at the cost of all others (so each were willing to put their lives at risk - because there is no other life), as we are left with no greater beauty than his holiness.

Indeed, Edwards will never let us alone, as this single demand is as demanding of the seasoned saint as it is of the suspecting seeker. "But many in these days have got into a strange antiscriptural way, of having all their striving and wrestling over before they are converted;

---

[108] WJE 2:95.

[109] WJE 2:274.

and so having an easy time of it afterwards, to sit down and enjoy their sloth and indolence."[110]

Chapter Summary

Many imagine Edwards as a curator, a gatherer and arranger of rare or endangered things. In his case those things would be a collection of colonial puritan thought. Instead he is better seen as an event planner who sits the right people at the right tables to facilitate the most meaningful conversations. He brings things, or ideas, together and proves their consistent relationship to each other.

By bringing Christian practice together with speculative theology, Edwards advances both. With the exception of his first and tenth signs of religious affection (the new sense and a symmetry of virtues), each is fairly simple.[111] Taken as concrete propositions, all of them are very practical. But, the operations behind these actions, the elements making them effective, are more nuanced. Practically, behind the practice of faith is the promise of change. Theologically, behind inclination is the ability to perceive. Here Edwards demonstrates that where a thing is true practically it is also true theologically, and the result is to push our faith into every academic and practical discipline.

To this point Edwards has brought theology to bear on practical Christian living. In the next chapter we explore how he introduces philosophy and science to the conversation.

---

[110]*WJE* 2:382.

[111]There is nothing new here. Selflessness, love for God's best qualities, eyes to see, humility, a changed nature, love and meekness, growth in a soft heart and desire for God, and consistent Christian behavior are all pretty basic Christian virtues. We do not need Edwards to tell us to do these things. We need him to tell us why Christians do them gladly.

Chapter 3

Our Context and the Affected Heart

EIGHTEENTH-CENTURY NEW ENGLAND was founded on Puritan idealism and order. Central to this was a model of a Christian community, which drew little distinction between civic and religious virtue. The family, church and political structure were integrated in a way that would confound most modern Americans. Each of these was connected to the others, serving its place in an organic system of hierarchical networks. From slave to child, to mother to father; from father to elder, to pastor to regional leader; from regional leader to proprietor, to governor to king; each member was a part of the other, and each dependent on those higher up. This created a happy and stable system, but like all cultural systems it also left room for periodic tension between competing, though mutually dependent, values. Managing these tensions was the responsibility of community leaders. A prime example, and one that would become especially troublesome for Edwards, was the question of church membership.

Classic Puritanism believed that the true church should be made up of regenerate believers and young Jonathan saw this model carefully applied by his own pastor father, Timothy. Timothy Edwards held to an exacting standard that required communicant members to give a precise account of not just their belief, or desire unto faith, but their faith itself. This account was then subjected to his own expert judgment for validation as a prerequisite to communicant membership. While Timothy was clear that no good work could merit salvation, neither could spiritual sloth be submitted as a means of grace. So, while godly habits could not be meritorious, they might still be essential, and demonstrable, as a part of a believer's preparation to receive the gospel. Put another way, clearing land, and plowing hard ground could not cause a seed to grow, but for Timothy, and later Jonathan, it was the starting point for any true spiritual farmer.

This set the stage for tension, pulling against the New England idea of a seamless Puritan society, where citizens were saints, and saints were church members. The result was a compromise, crafted in large part by Edwards's grandfather, Solomon Stoddard, pastor in Northampton, and it was crafted in a way that both demonstrated and established his personal influence in the region.

Stoddard's Influence

Solomon Stoddard began his Northampton pastorate in 1672 and over the course of the next sixty years rose to a position of such prominence that he was later described as the "Congregational Pope of the Connecticut Valley." It is difficult to overstate the influence of the community's spiritual patriarch, and as Stoddard's leadership grew to the regional stage his authority within the more local community became formidable. Marsden notes that in Northampton he "was revered and feared, sometimes loved, sometimes resented. His supremacy was unchallenged."[1] This influence allowed for the development of an extensive family network of influencers, including magistrates and clergy. Among these was his son-in-law, Timothy Edwards, Jonathan's

---

[1] George M. Marsden, *A Short Life of Jonathan Edwards* (Grand Rapids, MI.: Wm. B. Eerdmans Publishing, Co. 2008), 35.

father. It is likely, however, that the most influential in this family network was Stoddard's second son, Colonel John Stoddard. Colonel Stoddard was the town magistrate and took the lead in the region's military defense. As such he was the most respected judge in the region, and his patronage would later become important to his nephew, Jonathan.

So it was from a position of strength that Stoddard sought to relieve the rub between the battling ideals of a regenerate church membership and one that was also civically inclusive.[2] It is helpful to pause here and note that the latter was not a problem for the first generation of Northampton settlers. But, the beginning of Stoddard's leadership coincided with the rising of a second generation, and as is often the case, the second generation was less spiritually consistent than the first. At the same time, simply denying membership to less committed children would tear the political structure from its ecclesiastical moorings. The choice was between a pure church and a healthy society. And while the second could not be had without the first, it was unclear whether the first could survive without the second.

Many of the New England churches, Northampton among them, sought to stitch this tear by adopting the "half-way covenant." This allowed the children of baptized parents to be baptized without reference to their parents' salvation. The half-way covenant met the problem half-way. It allowed the children to enter as part of the covenant community, but it did not allow their parents standing in that community. In order to invite those parents into the church, and to some degree under the community authority, Stoddard went further than others, offering full membership to all adults who professed belief in orthodox doctrine and submitted to the discipline of the church. He did not require an examination in reference to their actual regeneration. The result was to increase both church membership and

---

[2] This inclusivity is less universal than what Mary Page's generation might value, but it likely has some of the same pressure points.

public unity, framing communion as a "converting ordinance" rather than spiritual meal reserved for the regenerate alone.

As pragmatic as this may have been, it would be unfair to describe Stoddard as theologically liberal, or even self-serving. Rather, by all accounts Stoddard's goal was set at the salvation and holiness of all under his care. In his *Faithful Narrative,* Edwards describes the town of Northampton as full of pure doctrine and careful thinkers, noting Stoddard's leadership as a foundational element. Edwards presents Stoddard's orthodox influence as the binding substance holding Northampton's spiritual life together. This became starkly evident when Stoddard's influence was finally removed. "Just after my grandfather's death,' he wrote, 'it seemed to be a time of extraordinary dullness in religion; licentiousness for some years prevailed among the youth of the town....There had also long prevailed in the town a spirit of contention between two parties, into which they had for many years been divided...they were prepared to oppose one another in all public affairs.'"[3]

Instead of signaling an element of liberalism, Stoddard's membership scheme showed him as "another kind of conservative, one willing to innovate in order to preserve what he believed to be the essence of Puritan tradition."[4] The question faced by Stoddard, and that would soon face Edwards, was how does innovation meet cultural/generational change in a way that honors the gospel? Stoddard was certainly practical, in a frontier-settlement kind of way, but he was also aimed at the hearts of his people. Indeed, Stoddard was among the most successful evangelists of his generation, and remembered as the first American to make periodic revivals a centerpiece of his ministry. His chief purpose was not church or community order, but the salvation of those under his care. It was toward this end that

---

[3] *Faithful Narrative,* as quoted by Patricia J. Tracey, *Jonathan Edwards, Pastor: Religion and Society in Eighteenth-Century Northampton,* Jonathan Edwards Classic Studies (New York: Hill and Wang, 1980) 72.

[4] Marsden, *A Short Life of Jonathan Edwards,* 37.

Stoddard relieved the tension between the social interplay of the family, town and church by lowering the bar for church membership. This would be the same tension that would finally cost Edwards his pulpit in Northampton. But for Edwards the crucial tension would be larger, more foundational. Both would hover over the same questions of how does the church recognize true spiritual faith, or gracious affections, in a way that is evangelistically helpful and biblically accurate, but where Stoddard began with people, Edwards began with philosophy.

Jonathan Edwards's Foundations

As Timothy Edwards's son, and Solomon Stoddard's grandson, no one was surprised to see that young Jonathan had both a quick mind and spiritual sensibility. This, coupled with his being the only son of eleven children, served to make him the center of family attention. This may have also contributed to his later admiration of the Spirit's work in the women in his life. Since Timothy Edwards was often out of the house, working hard in his pastorate, and for a while as an army chaplain, he took a special interest in preparing his boy for college by careful direction to his wife and daughters. By the end of his twelfth year, Jonathan had mastered Latin and Greek and was ready for admission to the Connecticut Collegiate School. The Collegiate School had three locations, and under his father's direction Edwards chose the school closest to home. There Jonathan sat under the direction of a close cousin as his first tutor.

While Jonathan almost certainly pleased his father in his academic achievement, it appears that he felt less assurance of his own spiritual health. He clearly demonstrated a spiritual sensitivity, often responding to the periodic spiritual awakenings in his father's church, but he would later despair of the temporary nature of these halting affections. As he described later in his *Personal Narrative*,

> I had a variety of concerns and exercises about my soul from my childhood; but had two more remarkable sea-

sons of awakening, before I met with that change, by which I was brought to those new dispositions, and that new sense of things, that I have since had. The first time was when I was a boy, some years before I went to college, at a time of remarkable awakening in my father's congregation. I was then very much affected for many months, and concerned about the things of religion, and my soul's salvation; and was abundant in duties. I used to pray five times a day in secret, and to spend much time in religious talk with other boys; and used to meet with them to pray together.[5]

But he then goes on noting the weakness and self-driven nature of this affection saying: "But in process of time, my convictions and affections wore off; and I entirely lost all those affections and delights, and left off secret prayer, at least as to any constant performance of it; and returned like a dog to his vomit, and went on in ways of sin."[6]

In this we see two important dynamics at work. First, there is likely some portion of redacted memory, applying his growing idea of the "new sense" to his past experience. Second, we may also catch a glimpse of his father's disagreement with his grandfather over the issue of relaxed church membership. As Timothy held to the stricter standards for communicant membership (those allowed communion), Jonathan would be forced to examine his own faith in a way that has since become rare. This practice of examination would later become his central mission in reference to the revivals of the Great Awakening and a clear target in writing *Religious Affections*. Timothy's hammer of traditional examination and Stoddard's anvil of controversial innovation had crafted Jonathan and set him to ask after the nature of true affection for Christ.

[5] *WJE* 16:790.
[6] *WJE* 16:791.

Philosophical Foundations

For his senior year the "Connecticut Collegiate School" was consolidated in New Haven and re-named Yale, allowing Jonathan access to the college's newly acquired library. While there would later be controversy over the influence that some of these books might have on the students and tutors, with allegations of fostered Arminianism and Anglicanism, they were a treasure for Edwards. Yale, and its library, gave the young Edwards the chance to wrestle with the greatest minds of the generation. Yale "gave him access to books that were fomenting an intellectual revolution shaking the Western world at its foundation."[7] This foundation was, at this point, in the world of ideas. But as the tremors began to be felt in the structures of practical theology, Edwards stood as the man uniquely able to measure their depth, and move with them to find rare treasures of common grace shaken to the surface. This is most clearly seen in his interaction with the writings of John Locke and Isaac Newton.

Locke

Up to this point Puritan education involved a pedagogic formula linking disciplines and subjects in an intricate whole, finally culminating in the "*technologia.*" As Perry Miller describes, "Therein were laid out all things, concepts, relations, propositions, principles, as in a graph which, with endless branches and subdivisions and 'dichotomies,' looked like a genealogist's diagram of some gigantic family tree."[8] The result was a scholastic web of ideas, theories and assertions that were, if not divorced, then at least estranged, from experience. It was a schematic drawing of an Apple Watch that had to be built before it could be worn. However, as Edwards was learning the technologia from his cousin and tutor Elisha Williams, he was also reading John

---

[7]Marsden, *A Short Life of Jonathan Edwards*, 18.

[8]Miller, *Jonathan Edwards*, 54.

Locke. The result was a contrast too stark to be either ignored or synthesized. In one hand Edwards held a static formulation of concepts, and on the other he held an invitation to empiricism, idealism and sensation. The result was to place him between his father's formula of required demonstrable spiritual experience and his grandfather's required correct behavior and agreement with a particular body of information. Edwards stood alone on this ground and particularly alone in his having developed categories and language to describe the difference between the two. The result was a departure from the technologia as, in the end, "Edwards' thought cohered firmly about the basic certainty that God does not impart ideas of obligations outside of sense experience, He does not rend the fabric of nature or break the connection between experience and behavior."[9] This was Edwards's Great Awakening; this was his revolution. This binding of experience to behavior may have been theoretical at Yale, but its implications would become awkwardly concrete in Northampton where pastoral decisions like who may receive communion and church membership were well beyond theory. These same issues were finally brought into an even sharper focus in his weeding through the conversions of the coming awakening.

For Edwards, information now comported with reality, and reality was met in the sensate world. "The universe is all of a piece, and in it God works upon man through the daily shock of sensation."[10] In other words, information, correct or otherwise, could no longer be disassociated from its reality in the world. It cannot be ignored any more than it can be known without being experienced. This would be the end of passive reception of information.

But Edwards did more than borrow or apply Locke, he advanced his ideas. Indeed in *The Mind,* Edwards proves both his genius as a philosopher and utility as a pastor by applying a more rigorous, full-featured empiricism. For example, one of Locke's important

---

[9] Ibid., 55.

[10] Ibid., 56.

contributions was to describe the distinction between an object's primary qualities, those indivisible from the object itself such as mass and number, and secondary qualities, or those qualities which must be mediated through the observer's mind or idea of them, such as color or odor. In this Locke was seeking to answer the child's question: when I see green or taste sweet do I see or taste exactly as you? To Locke these secondary qualities could be known only through the sensation of the knower. Edwards, however, went further, reducing Locke's primary qualities to the single concept of resistance, which he then demonstrated to be equally mediated through sensation. The result was to pile all of creation, and all of epistemology, into a single, sensational boat. Miller quotes Edwards saying: "The world is therefore an ideal one; and the law of creating, and the succession, of these ideas is constant and regular." Miller continues: "Such a sentence, rent from its context, so excited the awe of students that where Edwards is known as anything more than the preacher of hell-fire, he is considered the one American who saw through Locke's halfway, and half-hearted arguments, who roundly concluded that if color is subjective then so is mass."[11] The revolution was this: an object can only be known through the senses of the knower. Therefore, if an object is not known the fault is in the knower, not the object itself. In this sense the knower must have eyes to see or ears to hear, as the Spirit's work is indivisibly connected with a new way of seeing. It is important that Edwards was not suggesting an empirical subjectivism, but rather the opposite. A thing is what it is, regardless of the viewer's ability to see it as such. In order for the unseen thing to be seen the thing that must be changed is not the thing but the viewer.

The remarkable point here is not that Edwards was an admirer of Locke, or even that he improved upon his work in ways that would not be appreciated for another one hundred years, but rather that he did so in a way that honored and strengthened the boundaries of his Calvinism. As a Puritan, Edwards recognized the distinction between

---

[11] Ibid., 61.

speculative religion and living faith, and in Locke he found the same categories discovered and applied more rigorously. For one there was information and for the other there was information in concert with sensation. The result was a bombshell for Edwards, and finally, for practical theology as a whole.

The central question for practical theology is how to elicit and respond to affection. The problem is that people will have different responses to the same idea. For example, why is the gospel, or any particular portion of it, so exciting to one person and so unaffecting to another; or why can a particular song bring my wife to tears and leave me hoping they do not repeat the chorus again? For Edwards, the answer is found in Locke's assertion that a thing can only be known as it is seen by the perceiver. For Edwards as a man perceives so he is. In other words, a thing is not determined by our perception of it, but our perception demonstrates the type of thing we are. "If he perceives in a cold, dull, lifeless frame, the coldness is not in the inert object, but is his own."[12] On a practical level, this discovery allows a pastor to acknowledge that people can desire to desire something without desiring the thing as it is essentially in itself, and this is an indispensable category for any evaluation of spiritual health. It is also one that has been largely forgotten. Put in Edwards's later language, a person may have a speculative knowledge about the sweetness of honey, but this is not the same as tasting it himself. In the same way a person may have a speculative knowledge of God's beauty without a sense of it or of God himself.

A Few Words on "Sinners"

It is important to pause here to expand what we briefly referenced in chapter three. Ask almost any reasonably educated high school student what they know about Jonathan Edwards and they are likely to answer with eight words: "Sinners in the Hands of an Angry God."

---

[12] Ibid., 65.

This answer is more correct than they, or most of their teachers, would ever guess. If, as Edwards taught, hell is real and God is not bound by any 'half-way covenant," but instead free to elect those he would, then the preacher's task was simply to communicate to those who would hear in a way that conveyed the sense of his subject. And so, as we noted in chapter three, "Sinners" was not an exercise in theater, designed to elicit an emotional response, but rather it was an exercise in philosophy, or more specifically, epistemology, giving an empirical sense of the subject. In fact, Edwards's delivery was surprisingly simple.

> The way he delivered his sermons is enough to confirm the suspicion that there was an occult secret in them: no display, no inflection, no consideration of the audience. "Mr. Edwards in preaching," remembered one of the townspeople, "used no gestures, but looked straight forward; Gideon Clarks said "he looked on the bell rope until he looked it off."[13]

Instead, his primary concern was that of a pastor's call to communication, and in meeting this concern he had to step beyond ideas built upon ideas and unpack a more psychologically correct way of knowing. This is what he found in Locke. "If a sermon was to have an effect it had to impart a sensible idea in all immediacy; in the new psychology, it must become, not a traveler's report nor an astrologer's prediction, but an actual descent into hell."[14] If ideas are to be conveyed by words then words must create sensation and in this, Sinners was a turning point in philosophy. It is a popular introduction of sensate communication. If Miller is correct that "Edwards took each verse of the Bible as an object in experience" then "Sinners" is simply a public invitation to this same sort of biblical experience.[15] "Sinners

[13] Ibid., 51.
[14] Ibid., 156.
[15] Ibid., 48.

in the Hands of an Angry God" was Edwards bringing the university to the kitchen, modern epistemology to the pulpit. Emergent pastors appear to have done the same with postmodern epistemology, but there is a fundamental difference. Where Edwards acted, the emergents have reacted, beginning the battle having already conceded the biblical weapon of objectivity.

Newton

When the Collegiate School was finally reorganized in New Haven the principle tutors sought to modernize their curriculum as quickly as possible. Samuel Johnson noted that he and Daniel Browne took full advantage of the college's new library, introducing their new students to Locke and Newton, in particular. "They joined their utmost endeavors to improve the education of their pupils by the help of the new lights they had gained. They introduced the study of Mr. Locke and Sir Isaac Newton as fast as they could and in order to do this the study of mathematics.[16] There are also reports of Edwards having read Locke's *Essay Concerning Human Understanding* before this time, showing his uncommon intellectual independence. Regardless, it is clear that his experience at Yale was exceptional, especially considering that up to this point neither Locke nor Newton had been taught in any American college. In this his college years were extraordinary, as he was among the only Americans with the opportunity to explore both Locke's empiricism and Newton's metaphysic in the same sitting.

It has been argued, and sometimes rebutted, that it was through Locke that Edwards developed his idealism, and through Newton that he developed his naturalism. Considering Edwards's earlier interest in the natural world, and his witness to the experiential faith element of the church membership controversy, however, it seems that these two were as much partners in his discovery as originators of his thought. This does not mean that they were not crucial, but rather that they

---

[16] *WJE* 6:16.

helped him categorize and describe ideas he was already thumbing through.

Miller argues that New England Puritanism had "slipped" into the habit of treating faith as the condition of the covenant, and then making the assumption that faith was the "producer of the effect."[17] So, the tendency grew to line faith as a cause effect schema operating within a closed system. With Newton, Edwards undid the simplistic, observable metaphor, and though Newton may have stopped short, Edwards advanced his discoveries regarding matter and gravity in a way that left the system open, and specifically open to the Lordship of Christ.

Newton, as many before him, held to the idea of smaller particles forming the basis of matter. But the larger, and at that time unanswered, question was, how were these particles held together? Put another way, what was the final block of the solid nature of matter? Newton argued that the extension, hardness and resistance of any object were consistent with the extension, hardness and resistance of their smallest components, atoms. But if matter could be divided at an atomic level, then could atoms be divided further? And even more mysteriously, by what power did they cohere? As a scientist who disliked hypothesis, and as a Christian who feared reducing creation to a purely materialistic cause and effect, Newton declined to answer. Instead, "[h]e left his greatest discovery so wrapped in mystery that the only permissible conclusion was his 'Scholium' to Book III: the one cause which can penetrate to the centers of the sun and planets, that can operate not according to the quantities of the surface of particles (as do 'mechanical' causes), but according to the quantity of solid matter, must be God."[18] For Newton, it was enough to demonstrate gravity as the cause of celestial motion. It was also enough for many of his followers, since they shared his fear that any other answer would describe a world that was mechanical to the point

---

[17] Miller, *Jonathan Edwards*, 78.

[18] Ibid., 86.

of godlessness. Instead, they resorted to the medieval scale, weighing experience in reference to science at one end and magic, or in this case God, on the other. If, at the one end, the science end, gravity was inherent to all matter, and the cause of universal cohesion, then there might be no need for God at all. So instead they weighted the other end, postulating gravity as a law instituted and superintended by God, as his means of exercising his Lordship over his creation. Rather than science they answered with magic.

Edwards approached this subject as he did with all his best work; with careful definitions. Rather than considering an atom as an object, like a chair or a rock, he emphasized its quality, specifically, indivisibility. This indivisibility is then, for Edwards, evidence of stability designed by God for the exercise of his power.

> "The secret," cried the boy, trying at last to put it all into one searing paragraph, is that the true substance of all bodies "is the infinitely exact, and precise, and perfectly stable Idea, in God's mind, together with his stable Will, that the same shall gradually be communicated to us and to other minds, according to certain fixed and exact established Methods and Laws."[19]

All motion was then set in action amidst established stability toward a particular end. Things behaved in reference to their nature, or because of the types of things they were. In this thought we again see Edwards the Calvinist. Regarding Locke, he notes the variable as the viewer, not the object viewed. Regarding Newton, each object stood as proof of God's sovereignty as each was by virtue of its existence a continuation of his purpose. But it was still a type of thing and it operated in accordance with its type. With this settled, Edwards was free to go where Newton was not, postulating gravity as a function of solid matter. Matter's relation to other matter is viewed through its

---

[19] Ibid., 92.

gravitational reference, and this in a system fixed and set in motion by God's sovereign decree. As Wallace notes,

> Although Edwards arrived at the one conviction by argument and the other through a spiritual experience, his belief that God is sovereign in the physical order of the world remained as unshakeable as his acceptance of the doctrine of God's sovereignty in the moral and spiritual order. Many of the developments of his later thought may be seen as efforts to define the constitution of these two orders, and to show the manner of their dependence upon divine providence.[20]

The point is that regardless of his emphasis on systematization and categories, Edwards refused to pit any category against another. Instead, Edwards sought a unity in his thought, and refused to see one truth as a threat to another. "He is the last great American, perhaps the last European, for whom there could be no warfare between religion and science, or between ethics and nature. He was incapable of accepting Christianity and physics on separate premises."[21] As the worldview was in the midst of a massive shift toward the Enlightenment he responded by fearlessly supposing unity of thought and truth. This is the same unity so desperately sought by many younger evangelicals.

Other Cultural Changes

The ground of the university was shaking, both philosophically and scientifically. The world was moving as the Enlightenment began to drop ripening fruit in the new world. While Yale was ahead of the curve, it was only slightly so, and what is thrown in the classroom

[20] *WJE* 6:28.
[21] Miller, *Jonathan Edwards,* 72.

always lands in the pulpit. Edwards's brilliance was his confidence. He allowed himself freedom to explore new ideas confident that God's truth could not be undone by God's world. Therefore, Edwards was brave to apply science to philosophy, and philosophy to theology, and he did so with very little error. The next frontier was applying theology to people, and just as the university was moving, so were the lives of the people he was called to serve.

In May of 1735 Edwards wrote an eight page letter to Rev. Dr. Benjamin Coleman of Boston describing and defending the events surrounding the revivals in the Connecticut Valley. After several revisions, this letter was published in England as his *Faithful Narrative*.[22] The publication was met with enthusiasm and offered Edwards recognition on a larger stage, and in this it succeeded in Edwards's goal of legitimizing the sometimes emotional, often misunderstood, events of the Awakening. Additionally, it is useful for our purposes in that it provides a succinct description of the town, as well as the larger New England culture, at the time of Edwards's work. Among the most notable features of the Northampton community was an increasing moral tension between the young people and their town, family and church. Speaking of the few years between Stoddard's death and the Great Awakening, Edwards describes the young people of his community noting that

> The greater part seemed to be at that time very insensible of the things of religion, and engaged in other cares and pursuits. Just after my grandfather's death, it seemed to be a time of extraordinary dullness in religion: licentiousness for some years greatly prevailed among the youth of the town; they were many of them very much addicted to night-walking, and frequenting the tavern, and lewd practices, wherein some, by their example exceedingly corrupted others. It was their manner very frequently to

[22] *WJE* 4.

get together in conventions of both sexes, for mirth and jollity, which they called frolics; and they would often spend the greater part of the night in them, without regard to any order in the families they belonged to: and indeed family government did too much fail in the town. It was become very customary with many of our young people, to be indecent in their carriage at meeting, which doubtless would not have prevailed to such a degree, had it not been that my grandfather, through his great age (though he retained his powers surprisingly to the last) was not so able to observe them. There had also long prevailed the town a spirit of contention between two parties, into which they had for many years been divided, by which was maintained a jealousy one of the other, and they were prepared to oppose one another in all public affairs.[23]

The picture is of a community of young people running loose as soon as the collar of Stoddard's influence is removed, and so Edwards notes these "other cares and pursuits" in reference to moral behavior. Additionally, there was rising class division among the Court (Tory) party and Country (Whiggish) party. But the issue was larger than these things alone. In the midterm it may have offered stability to tie the church, town and family together, but conflict in one was soon felt in the others. In this case the tension that was first experienced in the generational struggles within the family and town quickly spread to unrest within the church.

A Rising Generation

Many scholars have noted Edwards's emphasis on and success with the youth in his congregation. What is sometimes missed is that he was

[23]*WJE* 4:147.

not alone in this emphasis. There appeared to be a very broad concern for spiritual welfare of the rising generation as others joined Edwards in recognizing a decline in the Puritan ideal of a stable, structured and pious society. What is even more often missed, however, is that the challenges among the youth were closely connected to larger changes in the economic reality on the frontier.

First generation frontier families lived in a state of warfare. They battled untamed land and uncontrolled natives. Community was a matter of survival, as they banded together for protection, trade, and sustainable mass. Politics were centered on the town meeting with political and military leaders being sent to the county assemblies to make decisions. Family was centered on the father, who might then be called in to political or military action. Church was centered on its pastor, who was expected to give direction to politicians and fathers. This interconnected hierarchy was begun for survival. But once this need was met, or appeared to be met, it became a barrier to the young and ambitious.

As the second and third generations rose, and Stoddard labored to keep the thread from pulling loose on the church membership end, he was aided by continued, and at times increased, Indian tensions. These native populations found a natural ally in the French. The Indians viewed the French as a more manageable threat to their land than the English, and the French viewed the Indians as an important partner in defeating the larger English population. Moreover, New England could not help responding to France as a Catholic nation threatening its protestant flank. This wartime/frontier setting served to push the church and political structure together, making the health of each dependent on the other.

However, as Northampton prospered and the frontier pushed west they began to enjoy a thin, though important buffer from both the Indians and the French. The result was that the Puritan community was eroded by the transition from frontier conditions to economic diversity. The people moved from surviving attack to advancing as economic units. Better homes, less fear of attack, and even some luxury items imported from Boston become part of the average lives. The authority that once kept them safe was now less needed and the result was a growing individualism.

Family Tensions

Compounding the problem was the issue of decreasing available land. Family land could only be divided so far. In-town lots were exhausted quickly (Edwards's own in-town grant upon taking his pastorate was an exceptionally generous allocation). As a result, the youth remained dependent on their parents for longer than would have been the case otherwise. The land-rich frontier was gone and Northampton's rising fourth generation now felt pushed to make their own way, while still tied to their parent's land. As Marsden notes: "tensions were exacerbated by a gradual transition from the more communal and deferential standards of the Purtian era to the more individualistic tendencies of the eighteenth century and by the perennial questions of availability of land for the younger generations."[24] If there was no room for them in town, there could be no room for them in leadership, and where they could not lead they would not invest. As a result, their adolescent status was extended and on display in Northampton.

This changed the political process as the town government transformed from the provider of capital to the chief arbitrator in the competition over decreasing resources. The inevitable result was to further increase distrust of authority in general, and the political process in particular. The degree to which the church was a part of this process was also a problem. Additionally, as in-town land decreased families were forced to move further apart, undercutting the patriarchal structure. Land to the west could relieve pressure, but only by increasing the separation of frontier-bound siblings from their extended family-authority, the town and church as a primary community. As Patricia Tracy notes, "The family unit, often living at

---

[24]Marsden, *Jonathan Edwards: A Life,* 125.

greater geographical distance from its kin and neighbors, had to adapt itself to declining agricultural opportunities by preparing the young to endure prolonged dependence or to grasp new kinds of opportunities in a very individualistic fashion."[25] This individualism was a direct threat to the Puritan idea of community. People were rubbing against each other in ways that could not survive the frontier, and would not abide the current social structure.

Imperfect Solutions

In many respects, Northampton had less of a problem here than others. Tracy offers Northampton's relatively low emigration numbers as evidence. The reason for this was that in 1730 the Northampton proprietors and town agreed to subdivide 14,000 acres to their southwest. This mountainous area was not as desirable, and certainly not as fertile as that in the north, but it was still sufficient to settle the younger generation. This area, later to be called Southampton, organized its own church in 1743 and became its own town ten years later. Tracy goes on to note that the town was settled by younger men (average age of 33.5) and they were all descended from the original Northampton proprietors. In short, Northampton traded assets for stability (land for peace?), a process that would do nicely to relieve the immediate problem, but little to relieve the long-term anxiety over how to make room for the next generation. Another option for generational progress was for young men to become tradesmen. There was some promise to this path. As the town grew more affluent it demanded the goods that tradesmen would produce, and as other settlements were established Northampton rose to serve as a trading center. But, this also required capital outlay and so was a difficult road to economic independence. In the end, the transition to adulthood still revolved around the establishment of a family and either a

---

[25] Tracey, *Jonathan Edwards, Pastor: Religion and Society in Eighteenth-Century Northampton,* 93.

farm or established trade. Both a farm and a trade required capital investment, however, and as families grew the parents had less with which to settle their children.

As Tracy notes:

> Almost all of their sons, the young men who came of age in the Edwards era, would go through a rite of passage to adulthood that was quite different from Northampton's traditional pattern of household formation. Although 94% of the eligible grandfathers had received land grants, and 48% of the eligible fathers did so, only 1.3% (3 men of 236) of the native-born Edwards converts were given land by the town. Rather than receiving a symbolic stake in the community out of communal resources, signifying the interdependence of individual economic fate with the good for the whole society, and the extension of the individual's responsibility to provide for his sons into the wider community's ability to sustain its members, the young men of the 1720s and 1730s had to await inheritance from their long-lived fathers, find ways to buy their own homesteads, or emigrate and search for greater opportunities.[26]

The result was that Edwards's converts married three years later than their fathers at 28.6, indicating that they were unable to provide homes for their families. This extended dependence, again, would serve to increase friction within the home.[27] Compounding the problem was a general decrease in community wealth. Much of

---

[26] Ibid., 100.

[27] Tracy notes that of the 300 Northampton wills examined, very few break out of the traditional legalistic language of distribution to express some sentiment, but all of those which express hope that the children would live in harmony, or in charity toward their now widowed mother, were written after 1730.

the land had been farmed for four generations, and it was becoming less productive. The result was that sons waited longer to receive from their fathers' smaller lots, which were then less productive. Yes, the Southampton property was new, but also less fertile, which is probably why it was not settled in the town's early years. As a result, Southampton was a poorer community, likely accounting for there being no record of Northampton objecting to its separation when it chose to incorporate as its own town. In this fourth generation, the sons had to wait longer for independence, and when they got it, it often came with debt rather than wealth.

The point is that this rising generation had little opportunity for self-built investment in the community, and less opportunity for meaningful inheritance. Lacking these the youth were by far the most likely to be affected by economic change and create social change. This eroded generational trust served to dismantle both community and family authority. The result was to lay the foundation for a religious and political revolution, and only artful leadership could avoid either. In the end the political leadership failed, while the religious leadership, being somewhat less centralized, succeeded.

And so, Edwards found himself in the midst of change. Indeed, it was change that would finally be expressed in revolution. In this he was of a generation that would both think and do, and both of these dynamics were in view in his ministry. His thinking was prematurely modern, and his doing was in response to the irreversible, changing social circumstances. In any event there was a growing shift that could only be ignored with special effort.

Our Cultural Context

It may have been this social shifting that cleared the ground for Edwards to think carefully about the concurrent philosophical transitions. Even so, there are many who argue against his being so heavily influenced by contemporary thought, and by Locke in particular. As Stein wrote in his introduction to Conrad Cherry's work, "For Cherry there is no question that William Ames, Richard Sibbes, Thomas Shepard, and other Reformed theologians were substantially more significant for Edwards than John Locke and Isaac Newton. Edwards used the new philosophy of his day in the service of theology rather than as a primary pursuit in its own right."[28] But, in a sense, this question of primary or secondary influence misses the point. Edwards's contribution was not his dependence upon others but the way in which he addressed them. While so many (think Benjamin Franklin) responded by discarding the old, and others (think "old light" Presbyterians) by discarding the new, Edwards held the best of both in an exceptionally orthodox way. As Cherry himself writes of Edwards in his more recent 1990 introduction, "his philosophical musings on the functions of the will, the nature of virtue, and the purpose of creation – phrased though they were in an idiom foreign to the modern reader – were attempts to cast fundamental problems into forms familiar to the eighteenth-century thinkers." Edwards was eager to address his audience, and this audience was increasingly modern. The current church is no less eager to address its audience, and that audience is increasingly postmodern.

Modern and Postmodern

Asking when an epoch begins is like asking when someone fell in love. There may have been embossed events, but these were only significant because of what had come before and after, they were not true beginnings. So discovering the beginning of the enlightenment is tricky work, but one embossed appearance must be the writings of Rene Descartes (1596-1650). Descartes wondered at his friends doubting the common (pre-modern) epistemology and responded by entering their skepticism in search for a way through. This effort led him to what he believed to be the bottom of all knowing, "I

---

[28] Cherry, *The Theology of Jonathan Edwards*, xxiv.

think, therefore I am." The shattering hammer was that, for Descartes, knowledge was no longer based on God, but on the awkwardly fragile "I." It was a stunning statement of independence. Descartes's idea was to begin at the bedrock, what he saw as the only knowable thing, the self, and from that point to build idea upon idea until knowledge, reason, and God were indisputably established. The change was in the starting point, the evidence accepted, but not in the way it was applied. But the process itself was still built on the confidence that truth was knowable, and demonstrable.

Postmodernism is similar in its beginning. Like Enlightenment thought, it also begins with the "I," but it is a much lonelier "I." If on a community level we are shaped by our culture, or our place in history, then on an individual level we are also shaped by our personal stories, or the unique events of our lives. As unique as these are to us, so is our way of knowing; we can only know according to our shape, and our shape is larger than our making. Truth may be self-evident, but only to the self as an individual, so each "self" owns his own truth, individually. In this postmodernism is the ultimate Babel, where each person speaks a language that only he can understand, simply because he is the only one who has lived his life. The tautology denies argument. Transferable objective information is removed. The result is to shatter the footing for any authoritative truth claim. Each man becomes a universe to himself.[29]

The consequence is an existential isolation, as the signature quality of careful thinking becomes the independence of a custom-built worldview. It may be that we can influence another person in the way one planet's gravity influences another, but each person is still distinct and so left alone to discover, or even define, truth. Of course few, or technically none, are able to envision a truly unique God (nothing new under the sun), and so each person is left to cobble together their own inconsistent, though to them preferable, view of the world, as

---

[29]Universe, literally "one word" describes all there is. It conveys a sense of isolation.

they dig through their box of available ideas and preferences. This of course leads to an an explosion of ideas, that is both exciting and overwhelming.

Sadly, this Mr. Potato Head faith stands immune to criticism. In this world, truth is simply a preferable story, or as Brian McLaren has described it "revelation by conversation."[30] This view emphasizes the dynamism of revelation where truth is found by conversation rather than critical or linear argument. It emphasizes revelation "happening to us" rather than being given for us. The problem is that "us" is in the singular.

For the post-modern Christian this change in culture also requires a change in church. Christian leaders must therefore lead the church through a series of adaptations. This "process" has created an amorphous movement, as some church leaders adopted their own special blend of progressive and traditional emphasis. At the same time, this movement gained strong footing through the early 2000s because "it is bringing to focus a lot of hazy perceptions already widely circulating in the culture. It is articulating crisply and polemically what many pastors and others were already beginning to think."[31] Put another way, they were attempting to do for their friends what Descartes attempted for his. The result was a short-lived abandonment of traditional evangelical epistemology by many younger evangelical leaders known as the Emergent Church. The more recent result has been a careful effort to affirm truth as found in Scripture while also affirming a greater humility in our way of knowing. The first felt like unleashed embarrassment; a half-way covenant allowing accommodation. The second, what David Seel calls the New Copernicans, feels like genuine questions being taken seriously.

---

[30]Brian D. McLaren, *A New Kind of Christianity* (New York: HarperCollins Publishing, 2010), 87.

[31]Carson, *Becoming Conversant With the Emerging Church*, 13.

What Is/Was The Emergent Church?

The church grows best in neglected fields. It grows in forgotten cultural corners, away from the bright, favored center. From Palestine to the catacombs, from the New World to the third world, the church generally "goes to seed" more successfully than it can be planted otherwise. In this, believers have engaged culture in the same way a wool sweater engages a soft back, being best worn where the need is most felt. To do this the church must constantly reform, toward the gospel and for the culture. The problem comes when these are reversed: deforming toward the culture "for" the gospel. In both cases the healthiest church will appear as a protest movement, sometimes protesting against its own reversal. The problem is that protest and anarchy are on the same line.

D. A. Carson argues that the emergent church is also a protest movement, with many of the leaders coming from conservative, evangelical, and sometimes fundamental, churches. In particular, they seem to be protesting a simplistic reduction of the claims of Christ as toggle switches, yes or no behaviors or believed propositions. As Todd Hunter, former director of the Vineyard USA, has said,

> "Modern... attempts to tie each passage off neatly into propositional statements that capture truth are backfiring and emerging generations see through the charade of our modern forms of exegesis. We are not simply autonomous knowers given the ability to decipher truth for others. Jesus understood that it's not only the truth that changes us, but also the journey of seeing truth"[32]

Standing at the center of his objection is the phrase "truth for others," though it would be curious to ask if this position should be considered truth for us. Regardless, here we see that at the very heart of the movement is the question of authority. Assuming the emergent voice,

---

[32] As quoted by Carson, Ibid., 22.

Carson captures the reactionary tone of the position well saying, "if absolutism is the cancer, it needs relativism as the chemotherapy"[33] The problem comes when the movement neglects to relativize its relativism with a tempered commitment to the knowability of God. God talks a lot,[34] and to bury this in mystery and humility is to miss the point. We are humbled, changed and loved by what God communicates, not what he does not. If there is nothing to hear, there is nothing to share, nowhere to go, and nothing for the church to do, other than gather as an awkward aggregation of persons using the others as a resigned audience for descriptions of their self-referencing experience. As Kevin DeYoung has noted, "Mystery as an expression of our finitude is one thing. Mystery as a way of jettisoning responsibility for our beliefs is another thing. Mystery as radical unknowing of God and his revealed truth is not Christian and will not sustain the church."[35] As of this writing it seems to have not sustained the Emergent Church's experiment.

Among the most articulate, and perhaps most representative of emergent leaders is Brian McLaren. McLaren describes the cultural shift that was and is continuing to take place arguing that the church must shift as well. Since protestant denominations were formed on the wave of the enlightenment "each denomination made sense of Christianity within the lines and boxes of modernity. You might say they rewrote and rearranged the ancient 'data' of Christianity in a modern program..."[36] While this is worthy of careful thought, it does not account for the Reformer's dependence on Scripture, their commitment to making the text available for all believers, or most damningly, their own deeply moving and personal experiences of the beauty of God. Neither does it account for Edwards's later commit-

---

[33] Ibid., 32.

[34] Hebrews 1.

[35] Kevin DeYoung, Ted Kluck, *Why We're Not Emergent* (Chicago: Moody Publishers, 2008), 39.

[36] McLaren, *A New Kind of Christianity,* 8.

ment to apply the best and most recent scholarship in a uniquely Christian way. Regardless, for McLaren "This modern-to-postmodern transition, this colonial-to-postcolonial cultural shift, was a major obstacle in the path of (his) spiritually seeking friends, and it had become (his) own struggle."[37] The result was a search for "a new kind of Christianity."

For McLaren the emergent movement is indeed one of protest, even revolution. "Luther's ninety-five theses have completed their job. It's time for another tipping point; it's time, we might say, for a ninety-sixth thesis."[38] But there is an important difference between revolution and reformation. The reformers were moved by their conviction that the church had left its biblical moorings, while some emergent leaders are moved by their conviction that the church has lost its cultural relevance. While the Reformers responded to the dawn of the enlightenment, Edwards met and responded to its fullest bloom, and each did so in the same way. Without shorting the value of careful thought and learned ideas, each sought to shape the church with reference to a knowable revelation in the context of a moving culture.

So the question is what does a postmodern revolution within church walls look like? For the emergent movement, it looked indistinct and reactionary, as it was formulated as a direction, an "exodus" from modernism. There can be no defined destination because for the postmodern believer the ideal Christian life is dependent on an ever-changing culture rather than an unchanging authority. In place of the salvation event there is a salvation journey, rather than a search for truth there is a search for relevance, in place of discovery there is conversation. It is an epistemology of belonging, of social connection, and at its worst, of fear.

---

[37] Ibid., 9.

[38] Ibid., 17.

Another Take

The emergent church is easy to talk about, and difficult to define. This is because it was incredibly diverse. Some in it saw a need for the church to communicate with the postmodern culture, while others saw the need for the church to adopt the postmodern culture. Either way, postmodern epistemology was at its root, and this is a root that cannot produce a stem. It is more like a moss, covering and spreading where the conditions are the most suitable. This is not meant as a criticism. Rather it is a description of why it is so difficult to define. One author described trying to define the emergent movement as similar to nailing Jell-O to the wall. It congeals, but there is no solid center. There are as many descriptions of the emergent church as there are emergent believers; a decreasing number of both.

Indeed, the emergent church covers a broad range of theological positions. What most emergent pastors hold in common is a willingness to critique how churches engage postmoderns, both in our pews and outside our doors. On the far right we find people like Mark Driscoll defending orthodoxy, and at times critiquing the emergent movement.[39] In the middle we find pastors like Dan Kimball arguing for the Bible as an "authority" and a "guide" but one that must be approached as a narrative. "The Bible is an inspired story, not a math puzzle... we need to be good students and really listen to what we

---

[39]"In the mid-1990s I was part of what is now known as the Emerging Church and spent some time traveling the country to speak on the emerging church in the emerging culture on a team put together by Leadership Network called the Young Leader Network. But, I eventually had to distance myself from the Emergent stream of the network because friends like Brian McLaren and Doug Pagitt began pushing a theological agenda that greatly troubled me. Examples include referring to God as a chick, questioning God's sovereignty over and knowledge of the future, denial of the substitutionary atonement at the cross, a low view of Scripture, and denial of hell which is one hell of a mistake" (Mark Driscoll as quoted by http://en.wikipedia.org/wiki/Mark_Driscoll, Accessed 2/27/2012).

are supposed to be listening to."[40] This is well said, and quite true, but it is also incomplete. Something also needs to be said about the propositional nature of Scripture. Continuing to the left we find Doug Pagitt, who describes Kimball's reliance on the Bible's authority as a bit stifling, perhaps even quaint. Pagitt argues for a "different emphasis on where our authority comes from. I am not trying to say the Bible is not an important part of our faith and following, but Dan comes from a tradition that places near total authority on the Bible."[41] Pagitt continues: "I am intrigued by Dan's use of the anchor as a metaphor (for the Bible) for not 'drifting away from proper belief... I think the idea of anchoring is a great idea if one wants to stay in port" The strength of the emergent church is its conservatives, those who want to make the gospel understandable to postmoderns. The weakness of the emergent church is its liberals, those who want to make it consistent with postmoderns.

With this in mind it is helpful to consider Robert Webber's unique approach. Many have written on the emergent church, but Webber is different in that he approaches the subject as a matter of sociology rather than philosophy. First, by using the label "younger evangelicals" he has broadened the issue to the evangelical church as a whole, and narrowed it to those who would be most attentive to more traditional positions. His label also highlights two important elements of the movement.

First, many emergents continue to think of themselves as a brand of evangelicals. While some struggle to argue for the authority of Scripture, or even the claims of Christ, they continue to value each. Additionally, they place remarkable emphasis on reaching the lost. This brings the issue into the walls of our own churches and creates a special urgency. Webber argues that younger evangelicals are still attracted by absolutes, but they want to find them in ways that lead to authentic (individualistic?) faith. To him, the question plaguing these

---

[40] Webber, *The Younger Evangelicals*, 98.

[41] Ibid., 113.

believers is, "How does one move beyond the morass of rationally defended faith? How does one return to a faith that is authentic, fresh and passionate as the first love of a precritical faith?"[42] Following closely on this is the question of how the church of this pre-critical faith can then engage an emerging world of philosophical relativism. The answer for these "evangelicals" is a return to pre-modern mystery. For many, this is a recovery movement, a step back to an older position.

Second, Webber's description highlights the generational element of the movement. Edwards is often commended for his work with the young people in his congregation. While this was not as unusual as some have suggested, the amount of speculation and number of theories behind it stand as evidence that he placed noteworthy emphasis here. It may be that his growing up under his father's ministry, slightly removed, even partly estranged, from the power brokers of the family gave him an affinity for those left outside the meeting house. It has also been suggested that Edwards's own spiritual experience, so dramatically marked by his early years, or his relative youth in comparison to his predecessor, were reasons for his affinity with the young people in his church. Regardless, he was exceptional in his own youth and clearly valued the thought and commitment of the young people in his congregation. As a result Edwards was well positioned to see the cultural changes his congregation faced, and in particular the way in which the evolving economy and destabilizing social structures had their most direct effect on the young people in his church. In the same way today, new movements continue to gain traction with young people before their parents. Of course as a protest movement the emergents have plenty of the "reacting injured" of all ages, but it is the young people who are most often willing and able to cast off anchors.

In addition, by limiting his subject to younger evangelicals Webber is able to focus on the most immediate influences leading to the

---

[42]Ibid., 59.

emergent movement. He does this by dividing modern evangelicalism into three categories:

1. Traditional Evangelicals: Organized 1970-1980 and institutionalized 1970–1990. These find their influences in the post World War II culture.

2. Pragmatic Evangelicals: organized 1980-1990 and institutionalized 1990–2000. These find their influences in the revolution of the sixties.

3. Younger Evangelicals: (2000–present). These find their founding influence in postmodern, post 9/11 events.[43]

The first advantage of Webber's approach is that it is broad enough to extend beyond the dying emergent movement. The second is that it shows the most identifiable and immediate causes of the movement, specifically each generation's reaction to the one immediately previous. So, as the traditional evangelical has cut their theological teeth on liberal/conservative debate, marshaling facts and propositions as ultimate evidence, the younger evangelicals reacted to propositional statements as a tool of dying modernism. In the face of traditional evidentialist arguments, succeeding generations argue that "classical Christianity knew nothing of the concept of propositionalism as held by Christians after the Enlightenment."[44] Instead, they suggest that Scripture is best understood in terms of its general, sweeping storyline. It is the either/or schema that is the problem here.

One of the most distinctive qualities of the younger evangelicals is their understanding of the church. Webber describes this as a recovery of the visible church, with a renewed emphasis on mission and service. This is helpful, though somewhat incomplete. Postmodernism distrusts authority and truth claims, seeing each as a means

---

[43] Ibid., 44.
[44] Ibid., 84.

of exercising power. As a result, emergent believers tend to distrust organized church structure. In place of a called out community[45] the visible church is often associated with believers living in isolation and scattered through the world. Incarnational ministry is particularized to the individual, the bride of Christ becomes a collection of brides described as a single unit, while still living alone. Of course this is unsatisfying, especially to millennial believers who value community as the place where authenticity is practiced and experienced. And so the seed of the emergents' decline was in the center of their epistemology. Community requires a shared culture, even if part of that culture is to value diversity, and culture is difficult to maintain with universal disagreement over authority.

Emergents and the Bible

Webber argues that the genesis of the emergent movement is found in a desire to bring theology and practice together. I believe this is correct, and it is reflected in a hungry search for "authenticity." The question is whether this authenticity is an apprehension of an objective reality, as Edwards would argue, or a private experience disconnected from evaluation. Standing in the middle of these two options is the question of authority, or more specifically, the question of the Bible.

While there is a range of positions regarding the doctrine of Scripture among emergent leaders[46] John Burke seems to represent something of a middle ground when he says, "the test of our theology (beliefs) must be relational, not propositional.... Would the people I live with say I'm becoming a more life-giving person to be around? If

---

[45] ἐκκλησία.

[46] By definition there is a huge range among "emergent believers" on every topic. Where there is no communication there is only non-convincing discussion. Everyone is left talking to himself.

not, what good are our propositional beliefs?"[47] There is so much to like about Burke's test that it is easy to miss the problems in his first sentence. Specifically by defining theology as "beliefs," Burke makes the subject dependent on the believer's belief. *The* knowledge of God is reduced to *our* knowledge of God, and this is mere "belief," rather than apprehension. To use Edwards's language, it is inclination without perception, making it impossible to decide to what one is being inclined. Next, and I believe this is common within the movement, is an unhelpful distance between proposition and relationship. Rather than being on a continuum, with each being dependent on the other to produce true knowing, they are placed in different baskets all together, and the proposition basket removed from any corner that has anything to do with genuine experience. Continuing down the subjective row, Burke removes evidence of our knowledge of God or, "belief," from the objectivity of love evidenced by behavior, and replaces it with the way those closest to us feel about our behavior.

Burke is not alone in his tendency to make knowing a purely subjective process. In critiquing Mark Driscoll's more traditional doctrine of Scripture, Karen Ward takes issue with Driscoll's method of using Scripture as a key for interpreting Scripture. This bedrock principle of hermeneutics is founded on a commitment to the organic nature of the text, as well as its unique authority. Ward, on the other hand, argues for a collaborative effort, leveling the Bible's authority in relation to other partners in the conversation. "I reference Scripture as the 'big S story,' a founding partner in a relational dance, as my friend Rachel Mee Chapman says, 'in the overlap of text, community, and Spirit.'"[48] Here, Ward is establishing dynamic authority as an overriding value of the movement. Specifically, it is to assess person over proposition, or the Living Word over the written word. "I do not see proof resting in Scripture alone, but in Jesus himself (his life, death, and resurrection) as attested to in Scripture and as reflected

---

[47] As quoted in Webber, *The Younger Evangelicals*, 7.

[48] As quoted in Webber, *The Younger Evangelicals*, 45.

upon, wrestled with, and discerned within Christian community, by the leading of the Spirit."[49] Of course there is a lot to agree with in this sentence, but the problem is in what is not said. Specifically, it leaves no room for the Bible as having unique authority. Authority is pushed, again, to individual experience of the Living Word, as informed by community.

This is not to say that the Bible is not valued among emergent believers. Rather, it is given voice as part of a broader conversation. The biblical writers may even be an important contributor to the conversation, but the authority comes from the conversation itself, or perhaps more fairly, the authority of Jesus is known in relation to the conversation as a whole. McLaren describes this distinction as moving from understanding the Bible as a legal constitution to understanding it as a community library. "At every turn, we approach the biblical text as if it were an annotated code instead of what it actually is: a portable library of poems, prophecies, histories, fables, parables, letters, sage sayings, quarrels, and so on."[50] This is certainly helpful in pushing the church to respond to differing genres of the text. But the cost is too high. This position alienates the written word from the Living Word, who came to fulfill the law, and bent his life to the phrase "it is written." In other words, Jesus treated the Bible as a legal constitution.

McLaren, on the other hand, argues that the Scripture is inspired in a way that gives it a seat at the table, allowing it to stimulate conversation across cultures and history.[51] In this it may be inspired in a way that allows people to encounter God, but not in a way that is uniquely promised by God ("God breathed").

---

[49]Ibid., 46.

[50]McLaren, *A New Kind of Christianity*, 79.

[51]Ibid., 90–93.

And Now This

Young theological trends are like old soldiers: they never die, they simply fade away. There is no announcement, no eulogy; there is just a wandering off, at least that is the way the Emergent Church feels. Whisperings began in the early 2000's, and soon after some of the leadership began trying to revive the patient by means of autopsy. Even Brian Kimball, who introduced the phrase "Emerging Church" in 2003, began to back away from it in 2008, saying:

> "I can't defend or even explain theologically what is now known broadly as 'the emerging church' anymore, because it has developed into so many significantly different theological strands. Some I strongly would disagree with.[52]

Kimball's disappointment, his alienation from a now broader movement, was the result of values without boundaries. It was like a river without banks, or a sea without a shore. When epistemology is privatized you are left with as many standards, as many universes, as adherents. There is no rally point, no meeting on the green. There are just individuals chewing on lonely musings. This happening to the emergent church, and its threat to the larger evangelical church, is the result of what Charles Taylor calls the nova effect.

Taylor's starting question is "how there came to be an exclusive humanist alternative to Christian faith."[53] And now that it has come with such remarkable speed, how has it moved from the intellectual elite to the masses? Taylor explains that prior to 1500 people lived in a natural world that "testified to divine purpose," where God was seen

---

[52] Dan Kimball, as quoted by Url Scaramanga, "R.I.P Emerging Church," *Christianity Today*, September 2008. https://www.christianitytoday.com/pastors/2008/september-online-only/rip-emerging-church.html

[53] Charles Taylor, *A Secular Age* (Cambridge, MA and London: The Belknap Press of Harvard University, 2007), 299.

as the foundation of their daily society (political structures, church, etc.), and so all the world carried an "enchanted" quality.[54] When God was found everywhere it was difficult to imagine anywhere without him. But with the Enlightenment came a new sense of our place in the world, a new introspection that might be described as an enchanting of the mind corresponding to the disenchanting of the world. Truth is then found in the self, mind, or most basically in sensation. Using poetry as an example of sought meaning, Taylor explains: "We could describe the change in this way: where formerly poetic language could rely on certain publicly available orders of meaning, it now has to consist in language of articulated sensibility."[55] Communication, poetic or otherwise, is now only possible in the degree to which sensation is shared. Now that there is such a distinction between our minds (inner self) and the outer world, "the buffered self begins to find the idea of spirits, moral forces, causal powers with a purposive bent, close to incomprehensible."[56]

This is the problem that the emergent church and classic mainline denominations have sought to address, and both have failed. These groups have each defined the preferred frontier as self-exploration, and the epistemology of more recent younger evangelicals (millennials) is the result. But now these younger evangelicals have come far enough down the road to see what is around the corner. Some have responded by continuing on, which usually means leaving the church. These are the well documented "nones."[57] For them the church, or at least the sickly parts they have seen, has made itself irrelevant.

Others have responded differently. These are Seel's New Copernicans. They value lived truth and they are the product of the partial evangelical victory over the emergent church. They still have the same

---

[54]Ibid., 25.

[55]Ibid., 353.

[56]Ibid., 539.

[57]Those answering "none" on surveys asking for religious affiliation.

desires for authenticity and a lingering buffered self, but they are not usually hostile to external authority. Instead, they are cross pressured by living in a highly pluralized society and as a result they are in a unique place to recognize the weaknesses of the church as it stands in this cultural moment. Specifically they feel the cognitive dissonance of post-enlightenment left brained faith (dissecting the chicken to its smallest parts) while also feeling the brittle thinness of the emergent church's hunt for authenticity (living with the brainless chicken in their family room). As a result they are no longer comfortable pitting experience against reason, but neither have they found their way through the ambiguity. As Taylor describes,

> "in face of the opposition between orthodoxy and unbelief, many among them the best and most sensitive minds, were cross-pressured, looking for a third way. This cross-pressure is, of course, part of the dynamic which generates the nova effect, and more and more third ways were created."[58]

This creates an instability, but it also offers an opportunity. These younger evangelicals, those who have remained in evangelical circles, are both uncomfortable with non-experiential faith and unimpressed with where postmodern Christians have landed. So for now we need to stop trying to win the argument, affirm the difficulties and invite them into the discussion. We need to see them as a hidden treasure in church.[59] a sincerely calibrated diagnostic tool, We also need to introduce them to Edwards.

---

[58] Taylor, *A Secular Age*, 302.

[59] David John Seel, *The New Copernicans* (Nashville, TN: Thomas Nelson, 2018), 20.

Edwards and the Bible

Surprisingly little has been written on Edward's use of the Bible, but for our purposes it is enough to note that Edwards's dependence on the unique authority of the Bible is proven by the fact that his biblical writings compose the majority of his work. This is not because he was unaware of the challenges to the authority of the text. Indeed, colonial America was very much up to speed with the European issues of critical biblical scholarship and "self-consciously transatlantic in its orientation."[60] This was true of Edwards more than most as he took full advantage of Yale's new library, as well as the constantly circulating scholarly journals available. As Brown notes, approximately one third of the nearly seven hundred entries in Edwards's personal catalogue of the Yale library reflect in some way upon his interest in the integrity of the biblical narratives. That said, in the midst of the rising skepticism of the Enlightenment Edwards appears to have remained constant in his dependence on the unique authority of Scripture. As Nathan Hatch confirms, "Jonathan Edwards was relatively untouched by these changes. His lifelong pattern of biblical interpretation conforms closely to the precritical approach."[61] I would go further suggesting that even his (basically) postmillennial eschatology stands as evidence of his resilient optimism in an emerging Christian community breaking through the rising secular philosophical independence. He was very aware of the serious challenges to a traditional view of the Bible, and very confident in the final acquittal of God's word.

Douglas Sweeney describes the reason for Edwards's complicated position saying "He was a 'both-and' thinker: traditional and modern, partisan and ecummenical, critical and edifying, catholic and anti-Catholic...His biblical scholarship was shaped by both ancient and

---

[60] Robert E. Brown, *Edwards and the Bible* (Bloomington, IN: Indiana University Press, 2002), 1.

[61] Nathan O. Hatch, Harry Stout., eds., *Jonathan Edwards and the American Experience* (Oxford: Oxford University Press, 1988), 119.

modern values..."⁶² He was not afraid of critical scholarship because he had a second validating standard—beauty.

"Edwards often spoke of Scripture as the very 'Word of God,' and 'Emanation of his Glory.'" For this reason it could be described as the precious word of Christ because "It evokes in us a 'strange and unaccountable kind of enchantment."⁶³ This enchantment, this weighty glory was bound up in his first sign of religious affection: the New Sense. In this Edwards found an irrefutable internal proof, and in one sense he is following earlier writers' descriptions of internal and external evidence for Scripture. But his "internal" evidence is more thorough. He is not afraid of new critical thought because for the believer it could not stand alone. The believer has been given new eyes to see (perception) and a heart to love (inclination).

> Mere cognition is deficient when it comes to holy writ. Until the Word descends deep into the heart of the believer, bearing the passion fruit of love, it will not be understood. 'Was there ever an age wherein strength and penetration of reason, extent of learning, exactness of distinction, correctness of style, and clearness of expression, did so abound? Edwards queried his enlightened, modern readers. 'And yet was there ever an age wherein there has been so little sense of evil of sin, so little love to God, heavenly mindedness, and holiness of life, among the professors of the true religion.'"⁶⁴

Here is the question asked by the emergent church, and now being answered by the New Copernicans. Mere cognition is deficient. Left-brained-rabbit-dissection-reason alone is wanting. But so is right-brained-hopping-rabbit-individualism. It is the same point Edwards

---

[62] Douglas A. Sweeney, *Edwards the Exegete* (New York, NY: Oxford University Press 2016), 20.

[63] Ibid., 28.

[64] Ibid., 33.

makes in the first pages of *Affections,* arguing for both perception and inclination. But he did more than speak to left and right brains. He demonstrates to all believers, and now especially to cross-pressured New Copernicans, a healthy approach to Scripture. It was the same approach he took to Enlightenment thought in general.

Edwards's Response to Modernism

In an optimistic effort to reestablish cultural relevance the emergent church has adopted the subjectivity of postmodern epistemology. They have done this in reaction (protest) to the weaknesses of modernity, and enlightenment epistemology in particular. They stand in good company with those who have had the courage to confess that, absent an objective starting point, there is no way to render reason reasonable. As Josh Moody has said, "Nietzsche may have been one of the first philosophers to feel the dangers of modernistic nihilism and the lack of any 'God-hypothesis,' whether one believes that such dangers were his doctrine or his nemesis, but since him more have recognized the totalitarian potential of modernity, and its nausea of meaningless."[65] What they have sought to do at the end of the modern period, Edwards did more effectively at its beginning.

When confronted with the limiting objectivity of enlightenment thought emergent leaders reacted with an equally incomplete subjectivity. Edwards, on the other hand, sought to reform it by adding another leg to the chair, offering a more complete epistemology. Moody has broken Edwards's thought into four elements. The first is to reform the Enlightenment's foundation of reason by a more basic dependence on revelation. "Reason is only reasonable if preceded by revelation."[66] Second, Moody notes that for Edwards, reliable know-

---

[65] Josh Moody, *Jonathan Edwards and the Enlightenment* (Lanham, MD: University Press of America, 2005), 160.

[66] Ibid., 157.

ledge is always monist; it has an integrated quality. "Edwards defies the common division of the intellect into separate realms of reason and spirit, of secular and religious, of philosophy and theology."[67] As a result knowledge coheres, it hangs as a piece. "Reality is invested with a single truth because of the single character of God."[68] There remains an essential distinction between parts, but these parts relate to each other indispensably. Indeed, these very relations are essential to their being known themselves. If knowledge includes both perception and inclination, and inclination is the result of perceived beauty, and beauty is a matter of proportion or consent, then knowledge requires distinction between parts. Even so, all knowledge is a single piece, unified under the sovereignty of a single God. Following on this Moody notes the third element of Edwards's epistemology as "reliable knowledge is heart knowledge."[69] In this Edwards tempers the Enlightenment's rationalism with the "heart" and the revivalist enthusiasm with real knowledge. "It is rather the sum of all these to form the central disposition of the person."[70] The rationalism of the old lights, and the enthusiasm of the new lights are each tempered by the single action of the heart as it both feels and wills. In the end this is the whole of his twelfth sign. Finally, for Edwards reliable knowledge is "God-dependent." The Enlightenment's tendency to devalue spirituality is undone by Edwards's insistence that all things and ideas are dependent on God for their existence. Here is a remarkable meeting of unity and diversity in the object, knower, and means of knowing.

Of course this is quite different than the approach of the emergent church, and its want is the open door for New Copernicans. When Edwards was confronted with the Enlightenment he sought to re-

---

[67] Ibid., 158.

[68] Ibid., 158.

[69] Ibid., 158.

[70] Ibid., 158.

form it by welcoming "the discoveries of the new science within the framework that encouraged belief in the vital, present activity of the living God."[71] The result was to validate individual experience in the world of an absolute God. Where modernity deified individualistic logic, and postmodernity deified individualistic experience, Edwards allows both as relativized by the individual God. The very premise of *Religious Affections* is that not all experience is of God. At the same time there can be no real knowledge of God apart from experience. As Moody summarizes, "Edwards's antidote gives a means to experience the spiritual and a means to evaluate the experience."[72]

To make the point clearly, Enlightenment thought introduced a separation between experience and information, spirituality and rationality. It then chose information and rationality as authoritative. Postmodern/emergent thought differs in just one way. It chooses experience and spirituality instead. The two are the same in dividing the person, each choosing the other half. It is an ugly business.

Edwards's sense of the heart, on the other hand, imports information through apprehension. He avoids the mistakes of each by finding a more biblical anthropology. This allows Edwards to hold tightly to both the objective and subjective elements of faith. Faith can then be both correct and engaging, reasonable and attractive. His world provides for an objective aesthetic, and gives room for the whole person to engage the real God. Here is real authenticity. Moody agrees, noting that Edwards's response to enlightenment thought was not a "totalitarian metaphysical abstract, but the living God; where plurality does not lead to relativism but to beauty. Discordant relativism dances in concert to divine music."[73]

---

[71]Ibid., 159.

[72]Ibid., 159.

[73]Ibid., 160.

A Case Study in Application

We have seen that the emergent movement is born partly from a desire to bring theology and ministry together. In fact, the movement might best be understood as an evangelistic effort to make the gospel understandable to de-churched postmoderns. In any event, moving the conversation from the classroom and church pew to the coffee house and workplace has shaped the movement because for the emergents the battleground is in the real lives of real people. Edwards's theology shares this influence. In addition to being a philosopher, theologian, professor, and short-lived college president, Edwards was a pastor, evangelist and missionary. His ideas were tested by events, and most particularly the events surrounding the Great Awakening. It is here that the objective/subjective split is given familiar faces.

In June of 1742, James Davenport arrived in Boston, and with great bombast promptly pronounced all ministers "unconverted." Awkwardly emboldened, and clearly unbalanced, he took to marching into pastors' studies demanding that they, at that moment, declare if they were indeed saved. He was not well received. The result was to magnify the excesses of the now spoiling awakening, calling particular attention to untrained and unaccountable itinerant preachers who gladly measured success by an accounting of subjective, emotional experiences.

The more traditional old light pastors responded with an equally awkward objectivity. If Davenport demonstrated the discrimination of a wrecking ball, the old lights possessed the subtlety of a corpse, as evident in its stillness as Davenport was in his frenzy. They were best embodied in the person of Charles Chauncy. Apparently anxious to announce his premise, Chauncy titled his first philosophical essay, published in 1739, *"As Men are rational, free Agents, they can't be religious but with the free Consent of their Wills; and this can be gain'd in no Way, but that of Reason and Persuasion."* Having declared his position, Chauncy then remained quiet during Whitefield's early bombastic appeals to salvation. Soon enough, though, he began arguing more publicly against emotional and external signs of salvation. For Chauncy, the real evidence of salvation was not physical or emotional; it was the believer's more reasoned manner of life. "If you have not been terrified, do not fret, because many are redeemed by the love rather than the fear of God; positive assurance is seldom obtained, and many who have 'a sudden flash only, a mere sensitive passion,' are guilty of spiritual pride."[74]

Edwards responded at his Yale commencement address with *The Distinguishing Marks of a Work of the Spirit of God.* Here, Edwards challenged Chauncy, though not by name, maintaining the affirmative, and making Chauncy's argument more strongly than Chauncy himself, showing five signs of a work of God. He then demonstrated that these were each also attainable by sociological means alone. He cut the ground out from under them both, showing that these things were neither proof for or against a work of God's Spirit. By 1746, Edwards upped the ante, offering twelve signs that were "no sure signs" of true religion.

The point is that [75]Chauncy argued his case on the grounds of scholastic psychology, dividing reason and imagination. Davenport, and many of the more enthusiastic, often less trained, evangelists, reacted with more experiential accounting. Edwards held Chauncy in his left hand, and Davenport in his right, and said no to both by saying yes to each. He changed psychology by bringing reason and inclination together. This was his argument for the awakening, and his argument against it. Where reason and inclination were together it was a movement of God's Spirit, where they were separated it was not. Edwards appealed to reason and will together, not allowing one to contradict the other.

---

[74]As quoted by Miller, *Jonathan Edwards*, 168.

[75]Ibid., 177.

Chapter Summary: Back to the Bigger Picture

In the same way we have McLaren in one hand arguing for subjectivism, and the older evangelicals in the other, arguing for adherence to information. But in the middle we find Edwards calling us to both. This sense of unity is not unique to Edwards, but as a centered ballast in the midst of a wildly swinging pendulum it is at least exceptional. Here he stands as the antidote to both the say-a-prayer-so-you-go-to-heaven reductionism of the Webber's older evangelicals and the Mr. Potato Head individualism of McLaren's emergents. He cannot be crammed into either hand because the gospel is too large, too complete. Put another way, "a common pitfall in Edwards' scholarship is to squeeze most of him into either the spiritualist or the rationalist box; as Joseph Haroutunian remarked, 'those critics that have been impressed by Edwards's spirituality 'have done no justice to his intelligence, and those impressed by his intelligence have been impervious to his 'sense of divine things.'"[76] In fact, they miss the point entirely. Edwards's genius is the ability to hold God's objective rationality and our experience of that reality in a single hand. He has discovered a theology that is as complete as each believer: rational, emotional and spiritual together.

Epistemology's deadly pit is to divide the head and the heart. Modernism holds the head alone, and sinks to the bottom. Postmodernism holds the heart alone, and sinks beside it. Edwards holds both together and has a living, thinking faith that allows the heart to be ruled and set free by the Word. It is true enough for Calvin, and authentic enough for Caroline. But it is important to note that Edwards did this in an environment of philosophical and political revolution. Indeed, Benjamin Franklin and Edwards grew up under similar influences, but Franklin responded as a revolutionary, casting off faith and authority.

---

[76]Moody, *Jonathan Edwards and the Enlightenment*, 9.

Edwards, however, was no less an innovator, but he was an innovator in a way that moved toward faith. "His experience of intensely held Calvinism in the era of the cool reason of the Enlightenment resulted in remarkable creativity."[77] It is this creativity that is sadly lacking in the emergent church and hungrily sought by the New Copernicans.

---

[77] Marsden, *A Short Life of Jonathan Edwards*, 4.

Chapter 4
A Model for Application

THE EMERGENTS ARE RIGHT. We have crammed God's Kingdom into a say-a-prayer-agree-with-me-keep-'em-safe corner, and it has tainted everything. We do this for several reasons. Sometimes we love people and cannot help ourselves. Other times we love ourselves, and want to be correct (competent, able, and respected: victor in the truth war). But, we are not built for safety, and truth is better used for breaking chains than walking in security. The purpose of the church is not to keep members safe, even safe against falsehood, it is to equip and send. Sending is dangerous business. The question is how to get our churches out of the corner and, dangerously, into the world.

This cannot be done if the thing we know best is ourselves, or, with respect to Calvin, if we know ourselves alone.[1] Reformed theology

---

[1] In fact, Calvin would assert that we cannot know ourselves alone. "Our wisdom, in so far as it ought to be deemed true and solid Wisdom, consists almost entirely of two parts: the knowledge of God and of ourselves. But as these are connected together by many ties, it is not easy to determine which of the two precedes and gives birth to the other. For, in the first place, no man can survey himself without forthwith turning his thoughts towards the God in whom he lives and moves; because it is perfectly obvious, that the endowments which we possess cannot possibly be from ourselves.... In the second place, those blessings which unceasingly distil to us from heaven,

is God-centered and we must not do our philosophy differently than we do our theology. Sadly, we have followed Descartes and turned biblical epistemology on its head by defining ourselves as the single knowable subject, the starting point. Edwards stands to say, "No." For Edwards, the only real knowledge, the only Christian knowledge, is inclination, and the distinguishing mark of the believer is not that he finds God, but that he finds him beautiful. So the most effective way we can equip and send our people is to demonstrate the beauty of God. This is the single strategy. It is impossible to leave the thing we find most beautiful; we are tethered to it. Affection is a function of aesthetics. It is the difference in believing in God and loving him, and believing is never the same as saving, beauty-seeking faith. For Edwards, Christian living is a response to reality rightly seen. Where perception is possible, inclination is inevitable.

An Age of Opportunity

The youth room is a proving ground. Those who study faith sociologically will confirm that there are typical times for exceptional spiritual growth. Marriage, birth of a first child, career transitions, and serious illness are all events that cause people to pause and evaluate. More specifically, it is at these times that they ask whether the thing they find beautiful is enough, or whether there is a greater beauty available. These sorts of events introduce times that God commonly uses to draw us to a greater commitment. There are also times that people are more likely to exit the faith, times when something appears more

are like streams conducting us to the fountain. Here, again, the infinitude of good which resides in God becomes more apparent from our poverty.... We are accordingly urged by our own evil things to consider the good things of God; and, indeed, we cannot aspire to Him in earnest until we have begun to be displeased with ourselves..." (*Institutes* 1.1.1). Calvin's point is that God's beauty, the "infinitude of good," is most visible when placed alongside our weakness, but Edwards would add that the final object must always be God.

beautiful, more real, than God. Comfort, career success and social acceptance are typical examples of these things. High school is a common time for experiencing both.

Along with first curfews, first dates and first cars, high school is the time when early beliefs become first loves. Edwards recognized this and invested a remarkable amount of time in the young people of Northampton. Many churches have recognized the importance of these years and invested in their youth as well. But many students have adopted faith based on third party authority. They have experienced their parents experiencing God, and they are attracted to that. They trust in it because they trust in their parents. This is not a bad thing, but throughout it all the job of the Christian parent is to help their children transfer this trust from themselves to their savior. This does not discount God's real work in the lives of children, but rather acknowledges one of the ordinary means by which he brings that work to fruition.

Unfortunately this is also the time when we are tempted to hit them hardest with the say-a-prayer-keep-'em-safe religion club. The problem is that they cannot know the beauty of God in the same way they know that Columbus sailed from Spain. As a result, there is both an urgency and opportunity for the gospel becoming real in the lives of high school students.

Urgency

Older, traditional research and common opinion suggest that the first year out of high school is a time that young people broaden themselves socially and liberate themselves intellectually. Tim Clydesdale argues that the reality is more nuanced. Instead of intellectual engagement, teens are occupied with practical management of their daily lives. What they eat, wear and buy, with whom they play, study and sleep, and where they work, travel and party are the dominant questions. Clydesdale suggests that the answers to these wheres, whens and ifs are, to a great degree, determined by their previous life patterns.

> The first year out, rather than being a time when behavior patterns and life priorities are reexamined and altered, is actually a time when prior patterns and priorities become more deeply habituated. What the vast majority of teens focus on during their first year out is daily life management: they manage their semiadult relationships that now characterize their social interactions; they manage their adult freedoms to use substances and be sexually active; and they manage expanded responsibilities for their daily life, including money, food and clothes. This is the common experience... what differentiates them is not the colleges they attend, but rather their family, faith and community starting points.[2]

The point is that faith significantly influences their decisions while in college, but also that their faith is established previous to leaving home. The question for us, the one that Edwards answers, is what do we mean by "faith?" Clydesdale continues: "Asking incoming American college freshmen whether they 'have an interest in spirituality' is like asking a soldier in a trench whether he has an interest in world peace or an arguing spouse whether she has an interest in honest and loving communication." Of course they have an interest, but interest in general may not help without biblical categories to organize that interest. As Edwards would caution, their answers do not necessarily reflect on their experience of "lived religion." They are dominated by the immediate, and the immediate is dominated by the useful. For many, faith does not qualify as useful.

Graduating high school students have a generally positive view of religion, but they see it as good in the same way they believe vegetables are good for them, even as they walk past the collard greens on their way to a bowl of Lucky Charms. In college, or in a challenging high school class, they maintain their belief in God by

---

[2]Tim Clydesdale, Tim, *The First Year Out* (Chicago: University of Chicago Press, 2007), 49.

isolating it from their experience. This is actually quite simple for many, since they are following a life-long pattern. Clydesdale offers some clarity, noting that an especially effective cultural influence on students is a general distrust of large organizations. In a college setting this causes them to segregate their core beliefs from their immediate studies. Edwards would describe this same segregation in theological and philosophical terms, noting that typical high school faith is not effective because it is not affective, and if it is not affective, it is not useful. If there is only information, if there is no first hand appetite for Christ, Christian high school students will segregate their faith, maintaining it in an intellectual, speculative fashion. Lacking real perception there can be no real inclination. A healthy appetite cannot be ignored, but the "faith" of many students can. At the root of equipping and sending is the urgency to pique in students a hunger for God's beauty, not just information.

Opportunity

Every Sunday we fill our youth rooms with people spinning in circles, choosing which direction they will begin walking. They have good information, and now, in high school, they are deciding if that information is useful. They show up for Sunday School for many reasons, but most are there because their parents are either in a class in the same building, or in the Fellowship Hall drinking coffee with friends. The question is not whether they will show up, but what will happen when they do. There are three options.

First, they can receive information, and there is nothing wrong with this, per se. It is like they are building a future home, using beautiful plans and sturdy materials. But, until they take up residence, moving their whole lives into that home, it will remain a cold, useless structure. Another option is entertainment, usually in the form of emotion. This can serve a purpose too, but of itself it is likely to do more harm than good, since healthy emotion must be in reference to content. As John Smith notes, "An affection—love, joy hope—is first an inclination of will, *a response, not a reaction,* made by the whole person to a reality—God, Scripture, neighbor—whose nature and 'Excellency' have been properly *understood* by that person..."[3] Smith's point is that emotion apart from content cannot produce change, because it is contrary to the nature of the soul to love an object that is unknown.

Our third option is to show them information in a way that will produce love; to come at the heart by way of understanding. As Edwards wrote, that which would "induce the soul to love, must first be understood, before they can have a reasonable influence on the heart... nothing can come at the heart but through the door of the understanding."[4]

The remainder of this chapter is a five week Sunday School curriculum designed to meet this third option. It is aimed at bringing content to bear on the affective lives of students, so they may see the beauty of Jesus Christ. It is written with the youth of Trinity Presbyterian Church, PCA, in mind, but it is also designed to be transferable and adaptable for other settings. These lessons are intentionally not written in the style otherwise expected of a thoughtful book, but I would argue that doing so is one of the more thoughtful decisions of this writing, because this is where it matters. This is where we ask whether it really matters to the people we are called to serve. This is the test. There is no doubt that what you are saying does not match the real world when your class gives up being polite and just goes to sleep. And there is no doubt that you have achieved clarity when that one guy asks an unsolicited question. If you want to retain and

---

[3] Sang Hyung Lee, Guelzo, Allen C., eds. *Edwards in Our Time: Jonathan Edwards and the Shaping of American Religion* (Grand Rapids, MI: Wm. B. Eerdmans Publishing, Co. 1999), 3.

[4] From Edwards's Sermon, "The Importance and Advantage of Thorough Knowledge of Divine Trinity," Hebrews 5:12 *The Works of President Edwards,* 4 vols., New York, 1843, vol. 4, p. 5. This edition is also known as the Worcester Revised Edition, as quoted by Lee and Guelzo, *Edwards in Our Time,* 3.

grow younger evangelicals then practice by teaching your high school Sunday school class. What follows in this chapter is an outline of what this might look like.

At this point it is important to add an exordium. The church needs the gospel, not as a starting line at which we begin faith, but as the road on which we travel. When that road is paved beautifully, and carefully maintained, we can move with lightning speed. But the minute we veer onto the shoulder, the minute our message becomes, "try harder," we're done. This is especially true in working with our high school students, who are constantly told they have to be smart enough, pretty enough, athletic enough, skinny enough, funny enough, popular enough, savvy enough, disinterested enough, and successful enough to be okay. When we allow our students to approach their faith the way they approach their college applications we are allowing them to worship another savior. The gospel stands to say "No, you are accepted to this greater institution, this cosmic Harvard, because of who he is making you, not who you have made yourself."

Showing students this beauty must be at the core of our ministry. Edwards's contribution in *Religious Affections* was not in describing the gospel, but describing the results of having seen its beauty. His purpose was not to say what the gospel is, but rather to draw a distinction between believing it theoretically and being drawn to it as beautiful. That is the emphasis of these lessons as well, but it is an emphasis that will remain unintelligible unless it is beside the clear and liberating call of the gospel.

Week One: Introduction

Everyone grab a partner. Now each couple grabs another couple. This will be your group of four. Remember each other. You will be together next week, too.

Everyone close your eyes. On the count of three point to the leader of your group, and then open your eyes. The person with the most fingers pointing at them read Luke 2:41–51 and discuss: 1. What would your parents have said if you did this? and 2. What did Jesus' answer mean?

Jesus and His Parents

> Now his parents went to Jerusalem every year at the Feast of the Passover. ⁴²And when he was twelve years old, they went up according to custom. ⁴³And when the feast was ended, as they were returning, the boy Jesus stayed behind in Jerusalem. His parents did not know it, ⁴⁴but supposing him to be in the group they went a day's journey, but then they began to search for him among their relatives and acquaintances, ⁴⁵and when they did not find him, they returned to Jerusalem, searching for him. ⁴⁶After three days they found him in the temple, sitting among the teachers, listening to them and asking them questions. ⁴⁷And all who heard him were amazed at his understanding and his answers. ⁴⁸And when his parents saw him, they were astonished. And his mother said to him, "Son, why have you treated us so? Behold, your father and I have been searching for you in great distress." ⁴⁹And he said to them, "Why were you looking for me? Did you not know that I must be in my Father's house?" ⁵⁰And they did not understand the saying that he spoke to them. ⁵¹And he went down with them and came to Nazareth and was submissive to them. And his mother treasured up all these things in her heart (Lk 2:41–51).

Ask the group: Did anyone have any interesting answers?

It is helpful to have a little background on what is happening here. Once a year a large group from the village would walk to Jerusalem together to celebrate Passover. Then, they would walk back together. It was like a church picnic. Walking together, step by step, they made friends. During the trip they would spread out a little without worrying because they were with friends, who were all watching out for each other's children. But when they stopped for the first night, Jesus did not come find his parents, and Joseph and Mary realized he was missing. Speaking as a dad, I'm pretty sure they were torn between two emotions: fear and anger. Now add that they had to walk back a day's journey to get him, and then that they searched three more days to find him, and you can see how both fear and anger would be growing to an impressive intensity. You can hear both emotions in Mary's voice, "Son, why have you treated us so?" Luke goes on to say that they were "astonished" and "distressed," but there is something else here, too. She specifically mentions Joseph.

My first thought was that she was doing what lots of moms do. When someone is really in trouble they invoke the father, but she is not saying, "Just wait until your father gets here." He was standing beside her. She is referring to something different, and Luke gives us a hint to what that is. He tells us that they did this every year, but something about this year is different. This year Jesus is twelve. You see, at age twelve boys would enter into an intense time of apprenticeship with their fathers. During that year boys would spend almost every moment with them as they began learning their trade, and everything else. Now Jesus is twelve and Mary emphasizes the question of how could he do this to his father? This was the year that he should have been walking with his father. Mary says, "Why aren't you with your father, learning to do what you are supposed to be doing for the rest of your life." Jesus says "I was."

Ask the group: What do you think he meant?

The point is, there was a turning point when the things of Jesus' life and faith had to become his own. In that culture it was at age twelve. In our culture we've pushed that back a little. We've extended adolescence, through the end of our school years, and now with extended graduate programs and new health insurance rules, we have extended adolescence even further. But while we may have delayed giving you adult responsibilities, civically, God has not delayed giving you adult responsibilities, spiritually. Up to this point most of you have adopted a faith that has been, in a sense, second hand. You have trusted in God because you have trusted in your parents, or maybe the friend who invited you to church, and that is a good thing. It is the means by which God takes a young man or woman and grows them up to be strong in the Lord. That is the normal way that God sharpens our swords. But now, in high school, things are different.

Ask the group: "What are the differences between high school and middle school?"

We tend to think of high school as middle school with more freedom, but it is more than that. In high school you are playing with live ammunition. What you do matters. The grades and the choices you make stay with you. They become part of a more permanent record. The same thing is happening with your faith. The premise of this class is that you are in high school, and it is no longer okay to borrow your parent's faith. Just believing is not enough. Did you hear that? Agreeing is not the same as trusting; believing is not the same as faith.

Anthropology

Look at Romans 10:9–10: "if you confess with your mouth that Jesus is Lord and believe in your heart that God raised him from the dead, you will be saved. 10 For with the heart one believes and is justified, and with the mouth one confesses and is saved."

Ask the group: "What does it mean to believe in your heart?"

We tend to take people and cut them into pieces. There is the head for logic, the body for action, or pleasure, and the heart for emotions. That is okay. It is helpful to consider each of these alone every now and then, but we treat them like a family of brothers; they are related, but they are also independent. In particular, we treat our hearts like our little brother that we can beat up if he gets carried away, but the Bible is more nuanced. It shows that there is more overlap. Our heads, bodies and hearts are not independent siblings, they are parts of a machine, and when one part moves it affects the others, and more than the others, the heart represents the whole self. So, Romans 10 is talking about believing, but more importantly, it speaks of believing a certain way. It is interacting with ideas in a way that change the way you feel and what you do: if you believe in your heart you will confess with your mouth. If your heart is engaged you won't be able to shut up, any more than you can be quiet about your favorite song, or sports team, or new boyfriend. Any other believing is not real believing.

Let me give you a story that will give you a better feel for what I am describing. Notice that I said "feel" and not "understand." I have a friend named Dan who was a great swimmer through high school. He joined the team as a freshman, was issued the standard, awkward speedo, and was told everything he needed to know before his first race. Among this information was the strong encouragement to always double check that he had tied his speedo tightly. I think you know where this is going.

So Dan lines up for his first race, looks down to see that he had forgotten to tie his speedo, just in time to hear: "Swimmers ready... Go!" Immediately Dan knew something was wrong, and very quickly everyone else did too. I imagine the flip turn was especially awkward. Dan finished middle of the pack, after which everyone averted their gaze while he exited the pool. Before the race Dan believed that it was important to tie his suit. During and after that race, he believed it in a very different way. Believing in your heart is to believe something in a very different way.

Now, here is the reason I feel so strongly about this. This is the time when your faith must become real, or be exposed as false. Either of those options is okay, because it is better to know for sure, right? It is also the time that the same will happen with your friends. You will see people fall away, and you will see people come to faith, in numbers you may never see again. So now is the time that we need you to draw your sword and see what you are actually holding. It is the time to start fighting to advance the kingdom. That is what we are going to be talking about in this Sunday School.

Is anyone concerned? Is anyone standing there saying, "Look, I hear what you are saying; I might even agree, but that has not changed anything. You are telling me that I need to stop believing in God with my head alone, and begin believing differently. But, I don't even know what that means. And, I do not have a month to live on a mountaintop and figure all this out. I have homework tonight, relationship problems tomorrow and soccer practice in the afternoon."

I have some good news. Show EDS Commercial.[5] This advertising video depicts a crew building a plane while it is flying with passengers. The message is that God is building our faith and lives while we are living them.

Compared to the people God is making us, compared to what we will be in glory, we are pretty laughable—laughable, and treasured, and God will make us effective. But we'll get to that next week.

Leaders of each group of 4: close your group in prayer.

Why Did We?

If there is time after prayer, we will close with a "why did we?" The point is to honor the students as emerging adults and to teach them how to teach.

Ask the group, "Why did we start with you discussing the Scripture in small groups?"

People learn best when they already have an opinion about the subject they are learning. The questions are designed to get them thinking and forming opinions about the subject before we begin. The idea here is not for me to tell you what to believe, but for you to be inclined to it.

---

[5] http://www.youtube.com/watch?v=nwluv2i6k9c. Access date October 4, 2018.

A MODEL FOR APPLICATION

Week Two: A Tale of Two Prophets

Sit with your partner and tell a story about either your favorite person to spend time with, or the best sports play you ever saw.

Anyone hear any good stories? One more question for the whole group: what is the best scene in *Harry Potter*?

I bet that if I measured your heart beats and breathing rates, they would have gone up a little while you described these things. Why do you get so excited about these things when you talk about them? There is a difference between things you believe and things you love. I can believe that The Great Gatsby is a great American novel, but there are a lot of people out there who get excited when they talk about it. That difference is the distance between belief and love.

Close your eyes. Now answer this silently to yourself. Are you tired of just believing in God? Do you ever wonder if that can change? Okay, you can open your eyes.

Think about this. God has something more beautiful than we ever hoped for. He does not want you to just believe the right thing. He wants you to fall in love. Now if that is just information, your heart rate does not change at all. But if you love him, or are starving for that sort of love, your heart just picked up the pace... maybe just a little.

Most of us go around every day asking what should I do? What does God require of me? Am I allowed to date an unbeliever, is cursing okay, is "crap" an appropriate Christian expletive, can I drink if I do not get drunk? We are asking the wrong questions because these are questions about belief, not love. That is why Augustine said love God and do whatever you want. The real question then is not what am I allowed to do, but how do I make myself love God? How can I be more moved by what God is doing than I am about whether my volleyball or soccer team wins, or whether I get to eat lunch sitting next to my friend. One preacher put it this way, those who truly love, gladly obey. When we truly love then reading our Bible is not just another task; it is not like eating our vegetables, something we do because we are supposed to. It is like being a part of that sports play or spending time with that favorite person. Think about your coming to church not because your parents make you, but because you want to. Anyone tired of feeling like a hypocrite?

Balaam

Ask the group: Is Superman a good guy or bad guy? How about Wile E. Coyote? Good guy or bad guy? What about Britney Spears? Sometimes the question is harder to answer than we would like. Anyone know whether Balaam was a good guy or a bad guy?

Let me give a little background. Israel is wandering the plains of Moab shortly before Moses's death, and they begin having skirmishes with the locals. They defeated a Canaanite king; they defeated a couple of Amorite kings, and the Moabite king, Balak, starts to get nervous. So, he goes to Balaam, a local prophet, and asks him to curse Israel. Now here is where it gets interesting. God tells Balaam not to curse Israel. Did you catch that? God talks with Balaam. He is not a Jew; he is not one of God's people. He is the go-to guy for the Moabites. Even his name shows him to be a bad guy: it either means "glutton" or "foreigner." Scholars disagree, but either way it is not a good thing. He is not a good guy. He is certainly not viewed favorably in the New Testament. Peter compares the false prophets of his own day to Balaam saying,

> With eyes full of adultery, they never stop sinning; they seduce the unstable; they are experts in greed– an accursed brood! [15]They have left the straight way and wandered off to follow the way of Balaam son of Beor, who loved the wages of wickedness. [16]But he was rebuked for his wrongdoing by a donkey–a beast without speech–who spoke with a man's voice and restrained the prophet's madness (2 Pet 2:14–16).

But even so God speaks to him, and tells him not to go with Balak, and to not curse the people. So Balak sends another group, offering more: more honor, money, acclaim. And Balaam says the right thing.

> They came to Balaam and said: "This is what Balak son of Zippor says: Do not let anything keep you from coming to me, [17]because I will reward you handsomely and do whatever you say. Come and put a curse on these people for me." [18]But Balaam answered them, "Even if Balak gave me his palace filled with silver and gold, I could not do anything great or small to go beyond the command of the LORD my God (Num 22:16–18).

Good for Balaam, but not for long. In the end, Balaam went with them, and that is how we get to the donkey part we all know about.

> When the donkey saw the angel of the LORD, she lay down under Balaam. And Balaam's anger was kindled, and he struck the donkey with his staff. [28]Then the LORD opened the mouth of the donkey, and she said to Balaam, "What have I done to you, that you have struck me these three times?" [29]And Balaam said to the donkey, "Because you have made a fool of me. I wish I had a sword in my hand, for then I would kill you." [30]And the donkey said to Balaam, "Am I not your donkey, on which you have ridden all your life long to this day? Is it my habit to treat you this way?" And he said, "No." [31]Then the LORD opened the eyes of Balaam, and he saw the angel of the LORD standing in the way, with his drawn sword in his hand. And he bowed down and fell on his face. [32]And the angel of the LORD said to him, "Why have you struck your donkey these three times? Behold, I have come out to oppose you because your way is perverse before me. [33]The donkey saw me and turned aside before me these three times. If she had not turned aside from me, surely

just now I would have killed you and let her live." ³⁴Then Balaam said to the angel of the LORD, "I have sinned, for I did not know that you stood in the road against me. Now therefore, if it is evil in your sight, I will turn back." ³⁵And the angel of the LORD said to Balaam, "Go with the men, but speak only the word that I tell you." So Balaam went on with the princes of Balak (Num 22:27–35).

Isaiah

Okay, keep that in mind. Let's look at another prophet.

> In the year that King Uzziah died I saw the Lord sitting upon a throne, high and lifted up; and the train of his robe filled the temple. ²Above him stood the seraphim. Each had six wings: with two he covered his face, and with two he covered his feet, and with two he flew. ³And one called to another and said: "Holy, holy, holy is the LORD of hosts; the whole earth is full of his glory!" ⁴And the foundations of the thresholds shook at the voice of him who called, and the house was filled with smoke.... And I heard the voice of the Lord saying, "Whom shall I send, and who will go for us?" Then I said, "Here am I! Send me." ⁹And he said, "Go, and say to this people: "'Keep on hearing, but do not understand; keep on seeing, but do not perceive.' ¹⁰Make the heart of this people dull, and their ears heavy, and blind their eyes; lest they see with their eyes, and hear with their ears, and understand with their hearts, and turn and be healed." ¹¹Then I said, "How long, O Lord?" And he said: "Until cities lie waste without inhabitant, and houses without people, and the land is a desolate waste, ¹²and the LORD removes people far away, and the forsaken places are many in the midst of the land. ¹³And though a tenth remain in it, it will be

A Model for Application

burned again, like a terebinth or an oak, whose stump remains when it is felled." The holy seed is its stump (Isa 6:1–4, 8–13).

There are some remarkable similarities here. Both Isaiah and Balaam hear God speak, and they are both, at least in the end, given a tough prophecy. They also both see the angel. But there are some important differences, too.

Balaam describes a conversation: "And God came to Balaam and said, "Who are these men with you?" (Num 22:9). Isaiah describes a person, and gives an incredibly detailed description of his beauty (Isa 6:1,3). Scholars always stop and think carefully when they read of God being described as holy, holy, holy. It is the only place in the Bible where we see a word used three times like this. I am not sure of everything it means, but it is pretty clear that Isaiah is seeing something beyond description; he is seeing God's essential self. Balaam sees an angel with a sword. Isaiah sees an incredibly ornate vision. Balaam sees generality as it relates to him. Isaiah sees details as they relate to God. One hears things with his natural ears (a talking donkey, of all things). The other is struck with a new sense of God's beauty. One is information. The other is Christian experience. Catch that. Balaam was not a good person, and he heard God talk. It is possible to mistake information about God with an encounter with him. Something about this idea is very scary.

Don't get me wrong. I am not saying that information is not important. The point of Balaam is that information is not enough. Up to this point in your life we've been giving you lots of information. Now is the time for something else to happen. It is not that information is not important; it is just not enough. In fact, information is very important. Isaiah's experience is not just experience. There are words. He is given information. He is told what to do. He makes a decision ("Here I am, send me") based on information, but not information alone.

Ask the group: What else influenced Isaiah's decision? What else did he get in the Temple? He saw the Lord.

Look again at verses 9–13. Did you see what he is called to do? It is not a pleasant job. He is going to lose friends, position, comfort, maybe even his life. But he has seen something more beautiful than that. He has fallen in love with something he has seen. Something he saw was so beautiful that he could not help himself. Everything else may be good, but it is nothing compared to what he has seen.

Ask the group: What was the best toy you ever owned?

When I was a kid I had a red Fisher Price barn. It came with plastic animals, a little farmer man, and fencing I could put the animals in, but best of all, when you opened the door the cow would moo. It was a great moo. Some of you had this toy, too. I've seen them; don't deny it! It was the coolest toy in the world. In first grade I took it to school for show-and-tell. My mother warned me not to bring it, but I would not be moved off my point. It was the coolest toy in the world and I was convinced everyone would agree. That is not what happened. Everyone else had stopped playing with those toys about a year earlier. No one laughed, but they wanted to. The next show-and-tell I brought a football. It is not that I did not love my Fisher Price barn. I still opened the door just to hear the cow moo. But, I loved the approval of my friends more. Social acceptance was more beautiful than my barn.

The same thing has to happen if your faith is going to stop being your parents' faith and start being your own. You have to see God as being more beautiful than even your parents' approval.

How Do We Get It?

Christianity is not just about believing, or even doing, the right things. It is about seeing God as being so beautiful that he is better than everything else. For that to happen something about you must change.

A Model for Application

Show trailer from *Limitless*.[6] This movie trailer tells the story of a man who takes a pill and is able to access his brain's full potential. The greater hope is that the gospel makes us more by showing us a greater beauty than that of ourselves fully realized.

Did you hear what he said? "How many of us ever know what it is like to become the perfect version of ourselves?" This is Balaam's quest. It is the highest hope of the world. It is to experience the thing you love the most, you, in a way that you enjoy the most. But what if you are a jerk? You, having the ability to have the things that you want most, in your fallen state, is not a science fiction thriller, it is a horror film. Still, this movie made millions of dollars because we love the idea of being changed by something as simple as a pill. God has something very different in store, something much more. He does not want to make us the perfect version of ourselves; he is making us into the perfect representation of himself. And we do not get it by taking a pill. We get it the same way Isaiah did, by seeing God's beauty.

Do you want to know how to do that? There are a lot of ways, but there is one we see in this text. Look where Balaam is. He is in Moab, and look who he is listening to. He is listening to the Moabite king.

Now where is Isaiah? He is in the temple. Hear me here: I am not saying you should insulate yourself from your world. I am not saying that you should spend all your time at church, or even all your time with Christian friends. But I am saying that you need time with God's people, listening to them, seeking his face together.

In your groups of 4 answer this question: what things do you do at church that you do not do at school?

Now, in Isaiah's day what things happened in the temple that did not happen outside?

1. Public Worship. You cannot see the beauty of God alone. You need other people to show you facets of God's beauty that you would not see otherwise.

---

[6]http://www.youtube.com/watch?v=THE_hhk1Gzc . Access date October 4, 2018. Stop at 1:27.

2. Evangelism. There was a court for the Gentiles. The outsiders were invited in. In fact, remember when Jesus turned over the tables of the money changers? He did this in the Court of the Gentiles. He was very serious about not letting anything keep outsiders from coming to his Father. The point here is that God uses ministry and mission to show his beauty to his people. Do evangelism, with other believers, and you will see the beauty of Jesus working.

3. Sacrifice. This is the most obvious thing, and also the most important. The sacrifices that happened every day in the temple make two things very clear. First they make clear that your sin is very ugly. You take an animal, slit its throat and watch it bleed to death and you will be left with no doubt that something horrible has happened. Guys, our least offensive sin, the one that we think is not all that bad, is so horrible that it could only be demonstrated by a brutal death. But here is the other thing that Isaiah would not have missed. It was not his throat that was cut. Your sin is more horrible than you think. And, it is completely gone because of the sacrifice, the final sacrifice, the bleeding of our true savior, Jesus.

    I cannot give you a vision of God's beauty, but I can tell you that if you seek his face, and here I am suggesting you do it by being with his people, he has promised that you will find him. Tim Keller says that awareness of his absence is evidence of his presence. His point is that you would never be aware that you do not have him unless he was with you, poking you, making you want more of him. So, take courage. The fact that you worry that you do not have enough of him, that you do not see enough of his beauty to be changed, is proof that he has enough of you, and he finds you beautiful enough to guarantee that change will happen.

Why Did We?

Ask the group, why did we show a video?

The producer spent millions of dollars making that 2 minute clip. The sound, color, speed of action, all designed to make you feel a certain way. I cannot do that by just describing it to you. I am not that good a storyteller. Sometimes it is important to feel what we are describing.

Week Three: In His Image

Review

We've been talking about the fact that you are in high school now, and the world does not know how to treat you. In some ways it treats you like children, and in other ways it holds you responsible for what you do. The good news is that God is nothing like that. You are at the point now where you have to take ownership of your own faith. You are now at a place where you must either take hold of your own faith in an independent, adult manner, or come to grips with the fact that you, personally, are not a Christian.

Last week we looked at two different ways of knowing God. One is to know information about him, perhaps even information that you recognize as correct, true. That is what happened with Balaam. He had information. He heard God talk and all he heard was information as it related to himself. Isaiah, on the other hand, experienced the same God, and the same angelic host, in a very different way. The New Testament would say he had eyes to see. The difference between Isaiah and Balaam was not what they saw, but whether they saw. Balaam saw God in a "natural" way, and the result was to believe something to be true. Isaiah saw God in a "spiritual" way, and the result was revolutionary. It did not just change Isaiah, it changed the nation, and ultimately it changed the world. If we get a hold of this idea we will have gotten a hold of something very important.

Do you remember the turning point in Balaam's story? Balaam spoke with God. He heard God's word, but there was a place when the donkey saw the angel and Balaam could not. The defect was not in what was available to be seen, but in what Balaam was able to see. One of the characteristics of a Christian is that he has been changed. This is what Paul said: "Therefore, if anyone is in Christ, he is a new creation. The old has passed away; behold, the new has come" (2 Cor 5:17). A Christian is someone who has gone from being one sort of thing to being another. He is a new creation. Jesus describes it as being "born again," and it changes everything. One of the important changes is that it makes you able to see God in a different way.

Nicodemus

> Now there was a man of the Pharisees named Nicodemus, a ruler of the Jews. ²This man came to Jesus by night and said to him, "Rabbi, we know that you are a teacher come from God, for no one can do these signs that you do unless God is with him." ³Jesus answered him, "Truly, truly, I say to you, unless one is born again he cannot see the kingdom of God." ⁴Nicodemus said to him, "How can a man be born when he is old? Can he enter a second time into his mother's womb and be born?" ⁵Jesus answered, "Truly, truly, I say to you, unless one is born of water and the Spirit, he cannot enter the kingdom of God" (Jn 3:1–5).

A lot of people have talked about what Nicodemus meant with his question. One thought is that he was being snarky, but that does not really fit. It is a private conversation; there is no audience for Nicodemus to impress. I think that he really did not understand. This is a guy who was an expert and was successful doing religious stuff. He was a leader, he was a respected Bible scholar, he was politically connected, he was successful, and he had mastered external religion;

he was a Pharisee, after all. He is the senior class chaplain, the captain of the football team, and he had a scholarship to a great school. He understood the stuff to do, the stuff to believe, but he was completely dead in understanding truly spiritual things. Nicodemus was like Balaam. He heard Jesus, but he did not hear him spiritually. He heard what the words said but not what they meant. In the same way, Balaam heard God say that he had blessed Israel, but he had no idea what that meant. They were both operating on a purely natural level.

Groups of 4: Give one person in each group a piece of clove gum. Ask them to chew it and now describe the taste to the others in the group. Now give everyone a piece of gum.

Ask the group: Is there is a difference in understanding the description and actually tasting the gum? Describe that difference.

This is the difference between knowing about God as a child (second hand) and experiencing his beauty (first hand) as a believer. That difference is what you are made for: you are made to be Isaiah, not Balaam.

Groups of four: Tell a story about a time you achieved a long term goal, got a hard-earned "A" in school, made a varsity team, went on a date with someone, or finally broke up with someone. Was it everything you hoped for?

Ask the group: What comes to mind when you hear this list: Lindsay Lohan, Britney Spears, Michael Jackson, Heath Ledger, Anna Nicole Smith, Marilyn Monroe, John Belushi, River Phoenix, Jimi Hendrix, Janis Joplin, Jim Morrison, Amy Winehouse, Kurt Cobain?

These are people who were at the top of their game. They achieved everything they wanted. Every one was famous. I suspect every one could have retired if they wanted. They were the best at the thing they wanted most, and they were crushed by it. The thing they found most beautiful turned on them.

Show video clip.[7] This is a segment from the late night show "Conan" during which the comedian Louis C.K. talks about our impatience with new technology.

We are laughing because we've experienced this. It is not just that we are bored with good things; we are angered by them because they do not make us happy! You cannot enjoy the things you have because they can never fulfill their promise. So what about you? What are the things that you want the most? Is it to be a part of a particular group of friends, or have a particular boyfriend; is it an athletic accomplishment, or better grades?

You are made to be satisfied by nothing less than a relationship with Jesus Christ. Anything else will leave you feeling like Balaam or Nicodemus, or Louis C. K. having everything, but missing something you cannot put your finger on. There is a simple reason for this. Genesis tells us that we are made in God's image, and that means a lot of things, but one thing it means is that something in you is designed to connect with something in him, and cannot be satisfied otherwise. Until you are more excited about him than anything else in the world you will always feel Balaam's conflict. You are made for more than just believing, you are made for really loving, and when that happens everything changes.

How Does This Happen?

I said that when you become a Christian, you become something different. You begin to see that everything you see is not all there is to see. You begin to sense that the physical world we live in is intensely spiritual, and you are satisfied by nothing less. You stop being this guy. Show the scene from *The Matrix*.[8] This scene depicts the evil

---

[7] https://www.youtube.com/watch?v=ZqkZ1sBDJhg. Access date October 4, 2018.

[8] http://www.youtube.com/watch?v=Z7BuQFUhsRM. Access date October 5, 2018.

"Agent Smith" wooing a traitor by offering a life of luxury, though the traitor knows the comfort will be a computer simulated dream, with no reality beyond his imagination.

But how does this happen? How do you go from being this guy (the traitor), to being the hero of the movie, Neo? How do you go from seeing the world you live in every day, your friends, school, the stuff you want, to seeing the spiritual reality that is also there? How does the image of God in us, the thing we are created to display, get fixed? The first thing is to know that it can. Look at Nicodemus two or three years after his first meeting with Jesus:

> After these things Joseph of Arimathea, who was a disciple of Jesus, but secretly for fear of the Jews, asked Pilate that he might take away the body of Jesus, and Pilate gave him permission. So he came and took away his body. [39]Nicodemus also, who earlier had come to Jesus by night, came bringing a mixture of myrrh and aloes, about seventy-five pounds in weight. [40]So they took the body of Jesus and bound it in linen cloths with the spices, as is the burial custom of the Jews (Jn 19:38–40).

In chapter three he did not get it. He was blind. But now, we see a very different person. Before, he came at night, afraid of what other religious leaders might think. Now, he is coming very publicly, in the midst of a huge spectacle. It is an incredible risk, taken by someone who has a lot to lose. Before, he came as a leader, asking hard questions, maybe even pointed ones. Now, he comes as a follower, giving up every bit of his status. Cleaning bodies was women's work after all, and really the ugliest of women's work. This guy has changed. In chapter three we see a curiosity. He is asking, "Who is this guy? Do I need something more than I already have spiritually?" In chapter nineteen we see someone who is very different. I would propose that this change is the same change that should be happening to you as a Christian now.

Groups of 2: Tell a story about a time you went from hating something to loving something. What made that change?

Ask the group, anyone hear a great story? Do you see anything like that with Nicodemus?

I would add two things. First, there is one on one time. There is a personal encounter. Next, in the interval between chapters three and nineteen Jesus does a lot of teaching. Nicodemus gets a lot of information. Nicodemus has an encounter with Jesus as a person and he gets information about what he is there to do. Experience and information: these are the two elements of loving God. Knowing what gum is, and tasting it.

Ask the group: How do these happen in the lives of high school students? What is the best way for high school students to get information about Jesus, and the best way for high school students to have a personal encounter with him? What are the things that keep students from going there, from doing these things?

Why Did We?

Ask the group, why did we actually give gum?

It would have taken much less time to just tell you about my point. It would have freed me to give several more nuggets of information. So why take the time? The best illustrations always make people experience the thing you are illustrating. People agree with things they are told. They love and remember things they experience. Isn't that the difference between growing up in a Christian home, and being a Christian?

Ask the group, why did I ask you about how these things happen in the lives of high school students?

Never ask anyone a question about which they are not the expert. You guys are the experts on high school students. Don't miss that. You have expertise that the church leadership does not. That makes you part of the church leadership. We need you!

A MODEL FOR APPLICATION

Week Four: Increasing Hunger

The premise of this class is that now is the time for you to take hold of your faith as your own. Now is the time for you to start putting experience to your information. Do not get me wrong. Christianity is not less than correct information. You cannot love someone if you do not know anything about him or her. You have to know God as he really is, not as you might imagine him to be, so information is important. But information alone is not enough.

With that in mind we have been considering differences that will become increasingly true of you as you move beyond mere information about God to an authentic faith. So our first week we looked at Jesus as a young man, and compared the transition he made with the transition you made from middle school to high school. Week two we looked at two prophets, Balaam and Isaiah, noticing that you can know things about God, you can even know his will, and do what he says, and still be outside his family. Then last week we talked about the fact that we are made in his image, and that means that you will be satisfied with nothing less than an authentic passion for Christ. I want to pick back up on that this week.

Break into pairs: tell your partner about a time that you felt you did not measure up.

It took you awhile to think of a story that was safe to tell, didn't it? But I bet every one of you thought of three or four that you could not tell. Am I right? Do not tell anyone this. Just think to yourself, what is one area where you do not measure up, and are embarrassed about? Think of one story you were not willing to tell.

That feeling is a symptom. Everyone in this room knows that there is something in us that is broken. Something in us does not measure up, it does not meet the standard, and we spend a lot of energy trying to hide it.

Adam Exposed

Groups of 4: Read Genesis 2:21-25 and discuss what the last sentence means.

> So the LORD God caused a deep sleep to fall upon the man, and while he slept took one of his ribs and closed up its place with flesh. ²²And the rib that the LORD God had taken from the man he made into a woman and brought her to the man. ²³Then the man said, "This at last is bone of my bones and flesh of my flesh; she shall be called Woman, because she was taken out of Man." ²⁴Therefore a man shall leave his father and his mother and hold fast to his wife, and they shall become one flesh. ²⁵And the man and his wife were both naked and were not ashamed.

Ask the groups, how do most people feel when they are naked? Why do you think that is?

When someone is naked they are not able to hide anything. Think about the way you dress. Chances are you wear things that accentuate your best qualities, and hide your worst. We are experts at it. Just like some people wear base to cover acne, all of us have strategies to hide the parts of ourselves we are not proud of. Think about the way you date people. If you are a terrible athlete, you avoid dates that show that. If you are uncomfortable with the other gender, you probably avoid things that will leave you alone with your date.

The point I am making here is that the degree to which we are aware of something that is ugly in us is the degree to which we work to cover it up. As your faith becomes authentic, this will change... slowly. An unbeliever sees his sin and becomes desperate to hide it. A believer sees it and becomes desperate to have more of Jesus, because the believer knows that fig leaves can never cover his ugliness, only Jesus can do that. This is the quality we are talking about today. Authentic faith sees more and more of your own sin, and responds by wanting more and more of Jesus. You know that your faith is real when you are never willing to stay put. You want to have more of Jesus, because when you see something that is beautiful you want to have it.

Ask the group: what makes the iPhone better than the Samsung?

They pretty much do the same thing. In fact, I would argue that the Samsung does most things better. The iPhone has almost no free applications, its screen is either too big or too small, it is fragile, its GPS navigation is terrible (it is getting better), and it gets slower with every update. So why do people want them? The reason is very simple. It is because it is more beautiful. It is a remarkable combination of clunky and sleek. It feels better in your hand. Even the box is something you want to keep. When you see something beautiful you cannot help being drawn to it.

Stop here for a minute. Do not let that statement just go by. This is important; do you believe it is true? Have you ever gone to a museum and seen a beautiful piece of art, and then seen an exact replica for sale in the gift shop? Why do they do that? Why do people buy these prints? Because when you see something beautiful you want to own it. You want to have it become part of who you are. You want to surround yourself with it. Of course, you would rather have the original, but unless you are rich, the replica is the best you can do, so you buy it.

Has anyone here ever been to an amazing concert? Did you buy the over-priced t-shirt? Why? There are probably two answers. First, that shirt reminds you of a fantastic experience, something you might describe as beautiful. Second, you pay too much for that t-shirt because it shows everyone else that you are the type of person who goes to that concert. And to you there is something beautiful about having them see you that way. The point is that everything you do is driven by what you think is beautiful and what you think is not.

As your faith becomes your own, as you begin to see, like Isaiah, with a "spiritual sense," you will begin to see more and more how beautiful Jesus is, and you will begin to want more and more of him. You begin to want to have that beauty become a part of who you are—like the painting. Do not miss that. It is a very important spiritual law. By the way, this is the real reason to seek holiness in your life. It is not because you want to be justified; it is because you want to share, or "own," the beauty that you see in Jesus. The greater your spiritual health, the more you want to look like Jesus.

That is why the more you have of God the more you want of him. Enough is never enough. Jonathan Edwards put it this way: "'Tis the nature of a newborn babe, to thirst after the mother's breast; who has the sharpest appetite, when best in health."[9] The more healthy your faith is, the more real it is, the more you will find yourself wanting him every day.

Moses

> Whenever Moses went in before the LORD to speak with him, he would remove the veil, until he came out. And when he came out and told the people of Israel what he was commanded, [35]the people of Israel would see the face of Moses, that the skin of Moses' face was shining. And Moses would put the veil over his face again, until he went in to speak with him (Ex 34:34–35).

This is talking about a time when Moses was meeting with God while receiving the law. The thing I want you to notice is the preposition used in verse thirty-four. Moses would speak "with" him. There are lots of times we see God speaking "to" people, but this is different. This is a conversation. There are places that describe God speaking with Abraham, and Jacob, but they are always in a more veiled way. We see him speaking as an angel, or in the dark. For them he is always more hidden. There is an intimacy here with Moses that is special. It is something that we have not seen since the Garden. Moses, who is the one who wrote this account, is going out of his way to show

[9]WJE 2:377.

that this encounter is more direct than those of the others, and it was not the first time it had happened. Look back a little earlier. "And the LORD said to Moses, "Behold, I am coming to you in a thick cloud, that the people may hear when I speak with you, and may also believe you forever" (Ex 19:9).

Moses is describing something special, and it is not a one time event. His faith was in the first-person. It was not something Moses inherited from his parents. It was a first-person relationship, and for him it was like a drug. The more he got the more he wanted. Let me show you what I mean.

Ask the group: what are some things most high school students want from God?

In Exodus 32 we see that while Moses is having these conversations with God, the people have begun to worship another god, the golden calf. God responds, saying he will keep his promise to bring the people into the Promised Land, but he will not go with them. God says if I go I will probably destroy you for your continued sin. Instead, I will send an angel, who will fight your battles and ensure you receive the land. Did you catch that? This is the perfect religion, at least for most high school students. They get the land, they get the stuff, but they do not have the dangerously awkward presence of God. It is basically saying: you go to heaven, but you do not have to go to church, or read your Bible, or worry about any persistent sin in your life.

But now, look at Moses's response.

> And he said to him, "If your presence will not go with me, do not bring us up from here.... 18 Moses said, "Please show me your glory." [19] And he said, "I will make all my goodness pass before you and will proclaim before you my name 'The LORD.' And I will be gracious to whom I will be gracious, and will show mercy on whom I will show mercy. [20] But," he said, "you cannot see my face, for man shall not see me and live." [21] And the LORD said,

"Behold, there is a place by me where you shall stand on the rock, [22]and while my glory passes by I will put you in a cleft of the rock, and I will cover you with my hand until I have passed by. [23]Then I will take away my hand, and you shall see my back, but my face shall not be seen" (Ex 33:15, 18–23).

He could have had everything he ever wanted by just letting God send the angel to fight the battle. They would have had all the wealth they ever wanted. Everyone would have respected them; more than that, everyone would have respected Moses, in particular. He would have been a hero. It would be like being the ultimate wrestler on the mat, with a beautiful girlfriend, and straight A's, without ever trying. Instead, Moses chose to lead people who did not trust him, live a brutal life in a desert and appear to everyone around him as a complete failure. Then he would get up early, go out to a tent away from everyone else, and meet with a God who might justly kill him at any moment. Why would he do that? I'll give you a hint. It was not that he did not want to be comfortable, safe in the Promised Land. The reason was that he wanted something more. He knew he would be satisfied with nothing less that God's presence. And every time he got a taste of it he wanted more and more. That is the sign of authentic faith. The more you see of Jesus the more you want of him.

Let me give my favorite description of this. It comes at the end of Lewis's, *Voyage of the Dawn Treader*. The children have joined Prince Caspian and his party on a journey to find the lost lords of Narnia. Among these is Reepicheep, the military leader of the Narnian mice. He is a legend in the land and he has now joined this fellowship, this group of men, women, boys and girls who are on a mission. They have reached the end of their eastward journey, and are about to return to the comforts of home, and return to a hero's welcome. He has done everything anyone could ask of him, but he is not satisfied. He does not just want to accomplish his task. That is not why he came in the first place. He wants something more. He wants the beauty of Aslan's country.

> My own plans are made. While I can, I sail east in the "Dawn Treader." When she fails me, I paddle east in my coracle. When she sinks, I shall swim east with my four paws. And when I can swim no longer, if I have not reached Aslan's country, or shot over the edge of the world in some vast cataract, I shall sink with my nose to the sunrise and Peepiceek will be head of the talking mice in Narnia."

This is the appetite of every healthy believer. It is an appetite that grows through a lifetime of following Jesus, and it is one that is to begin for you now. Follow hard after Jesus, because the more you see of him the harder you will follow, because an infinite God inspires an infinite desire. Anything less is proof that a lesser god is at work.

So how do you do that? What do you do if you agree with me, but have no idea how to make yourself start the journey, how to make yourself want to want him? You do three things. First, pray that God would change you. The Bible says that a Christian is someone who has been changed. It says that he tears out our old hearts, hearts that are cold and hard, like stone, and gives us new hearts. So pray for him to begin that work. Look at John 7.

> [37] On the last day, that great day of the feast, Jesus stood and cried out, saying, "If anyone thirsts, let him come to Me and drink. [38] He who believes in Me, as the Scripture has said, out of his heart will flow rivers of living water." [39] But this He spoke concerning the Spirit, whom those believing in Him would receive; for the Holy Spirit was not yet given, because Jesus was not yet glorified.

Jesus told a group people at a big festival that if anyone is thirsty they should come to him and he would give them drink, and he would do it by giving them the Holy Spirit. He yelled this in a loud voice. He is yelling at us to come to him and to ask for what we want, to ask for him to change us! Here is the point. The job of the Holy Spirit is to make Jesus feel real to us. To take the Bible, and everything that God is doing in our lives, and to make it real. So pray; ask him to do this.

Second, you have to be with other believers. One of the common ways God makes himself real to us is through others. So come to youth group, connect with friends at Bible Study, and of course come to Sunday School. Whenever I meet someone who is struggling with faith, or struggling with the church, the first thing I try to figure out is whether they are struggling by connecting or disconnecting. Those who disconnect almost always disappear. So if you struggle with being excited about faith then decide to connect with other believers.

Finally, you have to be alone. What I mean by that is that while you need other believers to grow in faith, you also need some part of your faith that is you connecting as an individual. So if your faith is only about connecting with others then it will stop feeling real as soon as those other people let you down.

Let me illustrate it this way. I love going to dinner with Ann and a few friends. I love seeing the way she reacts to their stories, and the way she tells hers to them. I fall more in love with her every time we are with other people because I see parts of her that I do not see when we are alone. But I also love going to lunch with her alone. I love talking with just her about how we raise our children, or build our house, or make camp better. I need both: time with just Ann and time with her and friends, to really know her, to really love her. One without the other will never work.

So if you want authentic faith you have to be alone, you have to be together, and you have to pray.

Why Did We?

Why did I ask the question this way? "What are some things most high school students want from God?" Why not say "what do you want from God?"

First by saying "most high school students" I am not asking you to get too personal. This lets you say what you might be thinking without having to own it yourself. Second, by saying "some things" I am not asking you to think of the most important thing, just something. These two things together make it easier for someone to respond.

Week Five: Lack of Self Interest

Last week we spoke about the idea that your faith becomes your own, when it moves beyond being something that you believe because your parents believe it. It moves from being just information to both information and encounter. This is the difference between the counterfeit that the world is tired of seeing, and the reality of an authentic faith, and its result is something amazing.

[Show slides of "Freedom" by Zenos Frudakis (Installation Art, Philadelphia).][10]

The artist described this sculpture saying that he wanted to express something universal, and he felt that being free of the world's restraints hit the mark. What do you think? Do high school students ever feel this way? Do students ever feel like they are held back from doing the things they should be doing? What about making the grades you want? Do you ever feel like you do not have the ability? What about being the athlete you want to be? Do you ever feel like you have less talent, or size, or discipline than someone else? What about making the friends you want? Do you ever feel you lack the confidence you need to pull that off? Have you ever wished you could be someone else? Do you think Balaam ever wished he could be

---

[10] Images of "Freedom" used by permission of the artist.

"Freedom" by Zenos Frudakis (Slide 1)

Isaiah? That is part of what Frudakis is trying to express here. But there is something else here that I do not think he intended. Look at the first panel of this sculpture.[11]

Notice how static this first panel is (Slide 2). There is no movement at all, and the shape lacks personality. In fact, what you cannot see here, but you would see if you could see this in person, is that the artist has embedded other non-human, inanimate objects in the wall. There are coins, there is a cat, and there are other incomplete body parts. This first frame is a mummy; it is indistinct, subhuman, at best it is dead. Does this slide make you feel uncomfortable? It should. We are not supposed to see ourselves like that. It reminds me of last week's lesson on being made in God's image. Anything else is dead.

---

[11]http://dcmemorials.com/index_indiv0006571.htm. Access date January 3, 2012.

"Freedom" by Zenos Frudakis (Slide 2)

"Freedom" by Zenos Frudakis (Slide 3)

This frame shows progression (Slide 3). This is clearly a man, but what kind of person is he? There are no distinguishing characteristics. There are no arms. He cannot "do" anything. It is the idea of a person, but no one in particular. I think this is the most uncomfortable image in the series, because it is something we recognize. It is a person who is so constrained that he is not known for who he really is. It is like he doesn't even know who he is supposed to be, or what he is supposed to do, but he is still trying. Do you know anyone like this? I think this feeling is common in middle and high school.

Now there is some shape (Slide 4). There is a goal. It is clear what he is trying to do. He is reaching to be something different than what he is, but it is not clear if he will make it. It is like the dream when you are running but your legs feel like they weigh a thousand pounds. Of course, you finally wake up and realize that you could not move your legs because they were under the covers. I wonder how many high school students feel this way. You have something you are trying to accomplish, but it's still muddled with so many other demands from other people. Most of us are somewhere between slide 1 and slide 4. That is true of high school students, and it is true of most other people too.

Look again at Slide 1. Now you see the progression. He has gone from being one thing to another. It's a beautiful picture. But what does that look like in the real world? What would it look like if you went to school tomorrow acting like this was true of you?

Pass out paper and pencils. Ask each person to write three bullet points describing what it would look like if they lived like a new creation, free because they are not trying to please their friends, or teachers, or even their parents, because the thing they love more is God. Begin by giving two of my own as examples and assure them that they will only share them if they would like to.

1. I would work more consistently for camp to succeed, not just as a business, but as an agent of change in the lives of campers and staff.

"Freedom" by Zenos Frudakis (Slide 4)

2. I would read and write more consistently as someone who loves to study rather than someone who wants to complete a task.

Now write two things that keep this from happening. Some of you may have written something broadly generic, like sin, but I would be surprised if anyone wrote anything this specific and pointed. I bet no one wrote "selfishness." Two of the most fundamental qualities of our sin is that 1) it hides behind generalities and 2) it is always bent in on itself. It is aimed at its own benefit. One quality of authentic faith is that you stop wanting God for what he can do for you, and you start wanting him just because you want him.

Jacob

If you ever want to know what is important to a group, go back to its very beginning. Look at what qualities were evident then. If you want to know what America values, look at our founding fathers; if you want to know what the church is about, look at Jesus, and look at the patriarchs. If it is a healthy group, the values you see in its founding will still be evident. You are the same way. Chances are most of your values, your political views, and yes, religious views, are the things your parents taught you when you were very young. The point here is that we can see the most important elements of our faith by looking back at the earliest fathers of our faith.

What do you remember about Jacob? He was the one who wanted his father's blessing so badly that he conspired to steal it from his older brother Esau. You have to understand that in his culture the blessing always went to the first born, and it meant he got a double portion of the inheritance, and that he then became the leader of the family. They did it this way so the family wealth and position would not be diluted. But when you read the passage you also get the impression that there was more involved here. Jacob wanted the stuff, but he also wanted something else. The Bible tells us that Esau was his father's favorite; he was the man's man, the hunter. Jacob, on the other hand, hung around the tent with his mother. Jacob did not just need the stuff from his father; he needed something of his heart. The problem is that Jacob was so desperate for this that he would scheme, connive, lie and steal to get it. After he stole this blessing from his brother, his older, more athletic, skilled hunter/killer of a brother, he had to run. So, of course, he ran to his mother who told him to go to his uncle Laban's house where he lived for twenty years. During this time he fell in love, became rich, and was promoted as a leader. But all along, there was friction between Jacob and his uncle, until finally the day came that he had to leave, and there was nowhere to go other than home.

Do not miss this point. He was leaving Laban because if he stayed it would have gotten bad, and he was going home, where if he had stayed, it would have gotten bad. He had to leave, and he had nowhere to go. Jacob's life was falling apart. He was this guy (show slide 2). He had no options. He could not move.

Then we get to Genesis 32. Jacob gets word that his brother is coming out to meet him with 400 men. Now 400 men was a standard fighting party, so what he hears is that his brother is coming to kill him. He can't go forward, he can't go back, and he knows that the next day every conflict in his life will come to a head, and it is going to pop like an infected boil.

How Did It Come To This?

Now, remember how he got here. Jacob wanted his father's blessing even if he had to betray him. After all, Jacob never saw his father again, and he never saw his mother again. He wanted his father's blessing more than he wanted his father.

Now, finally we come to chapter 32.

> The same night he arose and took his two wives, his two female servants, and his eleven children, and crossed the ford of the Jabbok. [23]He took them and sent them across

> the stream, and everything else that he had. ²⁴And Jacob was left alone. And a man wrestled with him until the breaking of the day. ²⁵When the man saw that he did not prevail against Jacob, he touched his hip socket, and Jacob's hip was put out of joint as he wrestled with him. ²⁶Then he said, "Let me go, for the day has broken." But Jacob said, "I will not let you go unless you bless me." ²⁷And he said to him, "What is your name?" And he said, "Jacob." ²⁸Then he said, "Your name shall no longer be called Jacob, but Israel, for you have striven with God and with men, and have prevailed." ²⁹Then Jacob asked him, "Please tell me your name." But he said, "Why is it that you ask my name?" And there he blessed him. ³⁰So Jacob called the name of the place Peniel, saying, "For I have seen God face to face, and yet my life has been delivered." ³¹The sun rose upon him as he passed Penuel, limping because of his hip. ³²Therefore to this day the people of Israel do not eat the sinew of the thigh that is on the hip socket, because he touched the socket of Jacob's hip on the sinew of the thigh (Gen 32:22–32).

So now Jacob is alone. He has nothing. All the stuff is gone. He is at the lowest point of his life and what does God do? He kicks him in the gut; he attacks him. If we are not asking what kind of God would do this then we are not paying attention. This is not the way a kind person would act. So how can God do this?

Here is how. All of Jacob's life he was fighting for his father's blessing (the stuff he would give him), and his uncle's wealth. Now he is about to fight for his brother's position. But here, on the eve of this final confrontation he wakes up being attacked by God, and in the process of wrestling, of striving against him, he realizes that he is holding onto him. Jacob is holding God in his arms and as soon as he realizes this nothing else matters.[12] Jacob responds saying, even if I lose everything, even if I lose my life, I now realize that the thing I want most, the thing I must have, is you.

This may be the first genuine moment of his life. He stops fighting for what his brother has, he stops fighting for what Laban has, he stops fighting to have what God might give him, and he starts fighting to have God himself, and it changes him. "I will not let you go unless you bless me." I thought I wanted my father's blessing, and I was willing to risk my life to get it, but what I really wanted was your blessing, you in my arms.

Just Like Us

So much of what you and I do in reference to church is well-calculated selfishness. It is nice to be around believers. It is nice to sing praise choruses. It is nice to come to youth group, and Christmas services, and mission trips. It is nice to have people respect us as mature believers, even spiritual leaders, or at least good people. But the real treasure is having the beauty of God himself in our arms.

We even do evangelism in a way that fosters selfishness - theirs and ours. We invite people to become Christians so that they can go to heaven. And we invite them because their decision reflects on 1) our ability to persuade and 2) whether we are actually right about what we believe. But we are called to so much more than this. We are called to trust Jesus so we have Jesus. Look at how Paul put it.

> I have great sorrow and unceasing anguish in my heart. [3]For I could wish that I myself were accursed and cut off from Christ for the sake of my brothers, my kinsmen according to the flesh. [4]They are Israelites, and to them belong the adoption, the glory, the covenants, the giving of the law, the worship, and the promises (Rom 9:2–4).

---

[12]You want God to feel real to you? This feels real. There is a physicality that is almost offensive. A God in our arms is a gracious God.

Paul is willing to suffer hell if it would bless God and his purposes, if it would further the thing God had called him to do.

When Jacob had a real encounter with Jesus in the wilderness, and when Paul had an encounter with Jesus on the road to Damascus, they both stopped wanting God for the things he could do for them (they were both offering their lives) and started wanting God for himself. This is the mark of first-person faith.

How Do We Change?

How are we doing? Is anyone feeling uncomfortable? Here is the real question. How do we go from here to there? How do we make ourselves want God more than we want heaven? How do we go from this (show slide 2) to this (show slide 1)?

Look at how it happened with Jacob. "When the man saw that he did not prevail against Jacob, he touched his hip socket, and Jacob's hip was put out of joint as he wrestled with him. 26 Then he said, "Let me go, for the day has broken." But Jacob said, "I will not let you go unless you bless me" (Gen 32:25-26).

Ask the group: There are a couple of really strange things in these verses. Anyone see them? First, this man, who most theologians agree is God himself, does not prevail against Jacob. How can that be? One way we know that he is God is that he just touches his hip and Jacob is scarred for life. That word does not mean strike, or hit, it really means the lightest touch possible. So, with no effort at all he can crush Jacob. But he cannot prevail. Why is that?

If God had won the fight he would have lost Jacob. This is God becoming weak so that he could give Jacob the blessing, the thing he really needed. When Jacob saw God demonstrating his love for him by becoming weak, he was changed. He started to want something different. He stopped fighting to save his life and started fighting at the risk of his life. He stopped fighting to have his way and started fighting to have his God. It is in our nature to pursue the greatest beauty we see, and for Jacob that is God becoming weak to win us.

Where do we see this most clearly? Of course, it is God hanging naked, helpless, on a cross. The thing that is most beautiful to a Christian is not the beauty that he is saved, but the beauty of a God who would save, and would save this way. This is what changes him.

Let me end with a story. It is not my story, but it is a true story. Tony Campolo teaches sociology at Eastern University in St. David's, PA. He is this tall, goofy, balding Northeastern College economics professor, and it is important for the story for you to have a picture of him in your mind.

A few years back Tony was speaking at a conference in Hawaii. There was a six hour time difference between Hawaii and his home so at about 3 AM he gave up trying to sleep and found a little diner that was open for an early breakfast. While he was there he overheard two women talking about their night. To hear them talking, and see the way they were dressed, it was clear that they were both prostitutes. Tony overheard one of the girls, whose name was Agnes, mention awkwardly that the next day was her birthday. She then quietly added that she had never had a birthday party. After she left, Tony introduced himself to Harry, the owner of the diner, and asked if he knew Agnes. He said yes, she came each night about that time. Tony then asked if Harry knew any of her friends. He did, so Tony asked him to invite them to be there the next night.

Tony arrived at about 2:30 AM the next day and began decorating: crepe paper, balloons, banners; it took some time to prepare. Slowly others began to arrive so that by the time Agnes showed up at about 3:30 all of her friends were there to sing happy birthday. When she tried to blow out the candles she broke down in tears and had to ask Harry to help. She then asked if, instead of cutting the cake, she could just run it back to her place. She had never had a cake and wanted to look at it for a while. While she was gone there was an awkward pause during which Tony asked if they could all pray for Agnes. They did, and then Harry remarked that he never would have guessed that Tony was a Christian. What kind of church do you belong to, he asked. Tony looked him in the eye and said it is the kind of church that throws parties for prostitutes at 3:30 AM. At this point Harry became angry. He said "No you do not. That kind of church does not exist. I know it does not exist because if it did I would join that kind of church."

Do you see what happened there? At 3:30 AM, in a little diner, somewhere in Hawaii, there was a transformation, and it happened because a tall, goofy, balding guy thought that what Jesus did on the cross, what Jacob saw of him in the wilderness, was so beautiful that he wanted some of that himself. I guarantee you that Tony Campolo did not want to get up in the middle of the night, especially after a full day of speaking, with hundreds of others waiting to hear him bring his best the next day, and throw a birthday party. There was no way he could do that without losing a step the next day. It cost him something. The thing that brought the possibility of transformation to those people, in that tiny diner, is the same thing that brings the possibility of transformation into this room, right now. It is the image of a God who would become weak to win you. If that image moves you, if it makes you want to have some of that, then there is something in you hungering to move to first person faith.

Now I want you to sit facing your partner. I want you to pray for this person. I know some of us are uncomfortable praying out loud, so you can pray silently or out loud. I want you to pray that the things they believe about God will begin to feel real. I will close in prayer and then we will switch.

Why Did We?

Why do you think we broke into groups?

There are at least two reasons. First, it gives us all the chance to tell our stories. We can get to know a couple of people more easily than twenty. Second, talked last week about needing to be alone and together. This is a little practice for the together part.

Chapter Summary

High school students are not unique. They are just transparent, and so they are a good starting place for reaching the church as a whole. Like them, we need information presented in a way that is affective. These lessons are designed to meet this need several ways.

First, you cannot love what you do not know, so God's word is the primary content. Second, students are drawn into interaction with his word through their own experience. Most of the questions asked revolve around what high school students think. By discussing what they know best, certainly better than the teacher, they are given ownership of what they learn.

Finally, it is important to be precise in describing the use of illustrations. Where Edwards used the most current philosophy and the most available analogy to unpack Scripture, we have used the most current film, art and stories. The purpose is to bring God's word and the students' experience together through illustrations that pique sensation. When this is done well it will also capture their attention, though this is not the primary purpose. Instead, the purpose of each illustration is to show the beauty of the gospel. This is different than showing the gospel as beautiful, as different as the words "of" and "as," and the difference is important. Using an illustration to show the gospel as beautiful is classic bait and switch. It uses the illustration to cover the gospel with a more familiar story or image. On the other hand, using an illustration to show the beauty of the gospel should uncover it. This illustration will demonstrate something about the gospel rather than something that is like the gospel. The difference is an illustration that may change what a student thinks or feels (quite a feat in itself), but it cannot change what the student is able to think or feel. It is only God's word that can do that.[13]

---

[13] "...so shall my word be that goes out from my mouth; it shall not return to me empty, but it shall accomplish that which I purpose, and shall succeed in the thing for which I sent it" (Isa 55:11).

Conclusion

MANY PEOPLE WORSHIPING IN THE PEWS and doing ministry in the world have trusted something that is weaker than Christ. Until this changes, they will always find other things more attractive than the gospel. In the previous chapter we suggested that the church is designed to equip and send. The prerequisite challenge is to transfer and transform. If we are going to be effective in doing the work of the church then we must know what that work is for each person. The order is crucial; we must know our primary work for each person with whom we work.

The first step is to communicate a static truth in a way that changes the person who hears it. Edwards would add that if that person is not changed in his affections then this truth has not been communicated. It may have been clearly said, and sincerely agreed to, but there is never transfer without transformation. We cannot send those who have not been transformed because they have not been equipped. The church might choose to train an unbeliever to participate in some ministry, short term mission trips are a common example, but we must not lose track of that person as a primary target of the ministry. Active ministry can be an effective means of evangelism, or pre-discipleship, but the church cannot equip the dead, no matter how lifelike they appear. We cannot prepare somebody to give what they do not have themselves. The result of forgetting this, of losing track of who should be sent, and who should be shown, is a bland, passionless faith. It is easily seen in the lives of our youth, as well as our younger evangelicals, as they cast for something more "authentic."

In 2001, researchers from Notre Dame and UNC, Chapel Hill began a ten year project of what has become the largest survey conducted regarding American teenage religion and spirituality. The result is the National Survey of Youth and Religion, and some of their conclusions are surprising. One unexpected finding was a lack of family conflict regarding religion. In his summary of the study's findings, Christian Smith notes that three fourths of all adolescents consider their religious beliefs to be similar to those of their parents, with more noting affinity for the faith of their mother over their father.[1] Only six percent consider their faith to be "very different" than their parents. But thirty-seven percent of those who describe their faith as different from their mother's, and forty-five percent who describe themselves as different from their father's, report that their faith is extremely important to their daily lives. Smith goes on saying that the idea of the iconic rebellious adolescent is flawed. It is modeled on observations of adolescent psychological patients, since they are the ones most available for observation, and does not represent more typical adolescents.[2] Instead, Smith found that adolescents are "exceedingly conventional in their religious identity and practices. Very few are restless, alienated, or rebellious; rather, the majority of U.S. teenagers seem basically content to follow the faith of their families with little questioning."[3] At first blush this is an encouraging report, but Smith continues suggesting that there is no conflict because most adolescents feel that faith is "not worth fighting about."[4] High school

---

[1] Christian Smith, *Soul Searching* (New York: Oxford University Press Electronic Edition, 2005.

[2] Ibid., Ch. 4, 2414.

[3] Ibid., Ch. 4, 2427.

[4] Ibid., Ch. 4, 2516.

students are not exploring other religions, and they are not pushing back against their parents' faith because neither are worth their time.

The Cosmic Yawn

Smith continues: "The first tip-off to the largely invisible and background nature of religion in the lives of most U.S. teenagers is what they talk about in general, wide-open discussions as being most important, central, and interesting in their lives."[5] Here the discussion turns to school, friends, sports, and family. There is no passionate arguing over faith because there is no passion; there is no inclination because there is no actual perception. Tell a teenager that he cannot go to church and in most instances you can expect a mild reaction. Tell them they cannot see their friends and you will see something very different. When it comes to faith they may hear the donkey talk, but they have only heard words.

The problem is not limited to teens. They are simply more transparent than their parents.

> Adults in the United States over the past many decades have recurrently emphasized what separates teenagers from grown-ups, highlighting things that make each of them different and seemingly unable to relate to each other. But our conversations with ordinary teenagers around the country made clear to us, to the contrary, that in most cases teenage religion and spirituality in the United States are much better understood as reflecting the world of adult religion, especially parental religion, and are in strong continuity with it.[6]

---

[5]Ibid., Ch. 4, 2709.

[6]Ibid., Ch. 4, 3741.

The unchurched do not reject the gospel because it is unbelievable. They reject it because they just don't care. It is not that they need more relevant services or places that are "safe" for them to ask hard questions; it is that they have no hard questions to ask. Caroline, the seventeen-year-old Counselor In Training introduced in the first chapter, was not unusual. She was just honest.

The Need

We have a toggle-switch faith. We categorize people as on or off, believer or unbeliever, and there is good reason for this. There is a point at which a person is transferred from the kingdom of death to the kingdom of life, and this moment is crucial. It may be very dramatic, or uncomfortably subtle, but in any event it is definitive and real. In light of the range of beliefs represented by the National Survey of Youth and Religion, it is tempting to say that we need more categories, ways of describing people who believe but do not care, and ways of describing people who care but do not believe. But we must be careful to not allow descriptions to become categories, since categories beyond those in Scripture are likely to cause more problems than they solve. The need is not for more categories. The need is for a more exact description of saving faith.

The Solution

Here Edwards brings something we tend to forget: faith is more than subscription. It includes a concrete, sensate, element that is as real and as convincing as a punch in the face. It is sometimes more subtle, and sometimes less, but its reality is evidence that the toggle switch has been thrown. Edwards's contribution was to bring the philosophy that would raise the questions alongside the experience that was otherwise impossible to measure. The result was to carefully define traditional terms rather than create innovative categories.

Edwards lived in a remarkable time. His world vibrated with new philosophical ideas and groaned with sociological challenges. He responded by bringing the first to bear on the second, in a way that was exceptional. Rather than either rejecting or bowing to the best scholarship of his day, Edwards improved upon it. Rather than rebuking the youth for thrashing within their shrinking social structure, he moved toward them, placing a special emphasis here with his ministry. And by doing this he spoke convincingly to the youth, their parents, and the community leaders. All of this made him ready to meet his moment.

That moment was brought into sharp focus under the lens of revival. With so many swirling events, and so many strident opinions, Edwards lived in a laboratory for his best ideas. Like the soon coming political revolution, the present revival required ideas and action to meet on the same field. Consequently, the revival needed a man like Edwards, who was able to create biblical bridges between the newest thought, the strictest orthodoxy, and the most common experience. Edwards's unique contribution was that he did this in a way that was delicately different from synthesizing, or even holding ideas in tension. Instead he would hold each without losing reference to the other. As Myron Penner has said, "As a Calvinist theologian Edwards was careful to process revival in terms of the sovereign agency of God. As a pastor responsible for the care of souls, Edwards was motivated by a desire to discern and encourage a genuine turning.[7] The result was not a rejection of one, or a wash of the two, but a painfully exact treatise, inseparably stitching them together. This was Edwards's genius, and it may be best demonstrated in his dissecting perception and inclination, and reattaching them under the rubric of affection.

---

[7] Myron B. Penner, "Jonathan Edwards and Emotional Knowledge of God," *Direction* 30 (2007): 63–75.

This is a skill that we must recover, and quickly. This is especially important in light of other recent efforts to respond to our current philosophical and sociological context. The emergents have jumped in the experiential puddle with both feet. The New Copernicans are looking at the puddle as one of many options. Others have neatly avoided every puddle and narrowed the church's experience to the faint pleasantry of believing the right thing. The result of each is a generation of muted Christian belief.

Recommendations

The question for Edwards and the question for us is the same. How can a Christian leader facilitate change in affection founded in the particular beauty of God? How can we help others see God's beauty and each love him for it. Edwards asked this question in the midst of an emotional frenzy brought on by the Great Awakening; for us it is against an emotional stillness brought on by general boredom. Edwards had to steer; we have to put our foot on the gas.

For each, the answer is the same given to Timothy in Ephesus.

> I charge you in the presence of God and of Christ Jesus, who is to judge the living and the dead, and by his appearing and his kingdom: ²preach the word; be ready in season and out of season; reprove, rebuke, and exhort, with complete patience and teaching. ³For the time is coming when people will not endure sound teaching, but having itching ears they will accumulate for themselves teachers to suit their own passions, ⁴and will turn away from listening to the truth and wander off into myths (2 Tim 4:1–4).

Timothy could have simply read Paul's letter to his church. The point would have been communicated, in a sense. Instead, Paul calls Timothy to preach, to bring the word, to bear on lives, in a way that is more complicated than just reading. The remedy for false teachers catering to one set of "passions" is the truth, aimed at quickening another, and the way it is aimed is important. This is where Edwards's philosophy should change us. His challenge to us would be to listen to Caroline, and show her something more beautiful than her friends, family or school. We must show her that Jacob ran, wrestled, and limped for the rest of his life; and he also held God in his arms. Moses fled, led, and died alone on a mountain; and he also spoke with God face to face. David was promoted, demoted, and watched his family fall apart; and he also beheld God in his temple. Isaiah was burned, ignored, and watched Israel's defeat; and he also saw the Lord high and lifted up. Paul was mocked, beaten, and executed far from home; and he also saw the risen Lord. Each of these lived in a world as real, present, authentic, dangerous and dramatic as our own. Each felt the joy and loss of social acceptance, career success, family blessing and personal comfort, and each found something else even more real, more affecting. Edwards would challenge us to show Caroline something more beautiful than her self-imposed passions. He would also challenge her with the warning that seeing others see the beauty of God is never enough. We are changed by beholding him, not beholding them.[8] I also think he would have Mary Page head this committee.

Of course there are other fronts where the battle for affective faith can be fought, and so there is need for additional research. Three particular areas come to mind. First, while there has been some work done comparing Edwards to Benjamin Franklin, particular attention to contrasting Franklin's mere naturalism with Edwards's theologically charged interest in natural sciences might do for classic liberalism what his theology has done for postmodernism. Next, while this book has poked Edwards's aesthetic with reference to his *Treatise*

---

[8]"And we all, with unveiled face, beholding the glory of the Lord, are being transformed into the same image from one degree of glory to another" (2 Cor 3:18).

Concerning Religious Affections, a more compact treatment might be written with reference to his sermon *A Divine and Supernatural Light,* or a more complete treatment with reference to his work on the Trinity. Finally, a more ambitious writer might compare Edwards's interplay of ontology, aesthetics and epistemology with the Roman Catholic use of architecture (ontology demonstrated) and art (ontology accessed). But for those who do this, please remember to aim your work at the hearts of those of us in the pews, and the hearts of those outside the doors.

So go write, teach, preach for Caroline, for Mary Page, and for me.

VITA

Adam Boyd was born on July 10, 1965 in Atlanta, GA to Spencer W. Boyd, Jr. and Dorothy Coe Boyd. After graduating high school at Westminster Schools he attended Wofford College in Spartanburg, SC. During his freshman year at Wofford Adam's brother, Bobby, invited him to a "Christian Believers United" conference in Montreat, NC, where he received Christ and was changed. He was made a "new creation."

He graduated from Wofford College in 1988 with a Bachelor of Arts degree in Government and Religion. He received the Master of Divinity in 1992 from Reformed Theological Seminary in Jackson, MS and a Doctor (D.Min.) in 2012. from Reformed Theological Seminary in Orlando, FL.

Upon graduation from Jackson Adam moved to Black Mountain, NC where he joined his family in directing and operating Christian summer camps. In 1992 he became the Director of Camp Timberlake for Boys. In 2001 he and his wife became the Executive Directors as well as the directors of their girls program, Camp Merri-Mac. In 2008 they began a wilderness expedition program, Black Mountain Expeditions.

Adam is a member of Trinity Presbyterian Church in Asheville, NC where he teaches the high school Sunday school class.

In 1990 Adam married his favorite camp counselor, Ann Elizabeth Morrow. They have three children, Mary Page, Joe and Hank, and serve together as camp directors.

BIBLIOGRAPHY

Achtemeier, Elizabeth. *Nahum – Malachi.* Interpretation. Atlanta, GA: John Knox Press, 1986.

Alter, Robert. *Genesis.* New York: W.W. Norton & Company, 1996.

_____. *The Book of Psalms.* New York: W.W. Norton & Company, 2007.

Audi, Robert. "Postmodernism." *The Cambridge Dictionary of Philosophy.* Cambridge: Cambridge University Press, 1995.

Barrett, C.K. *The Second Epistle to the Corinthians.* Black's New Testament Commentary. Peabody, MA: Hendrickson Publishing, 1973.

Behm, Johannes. Καρδία in *Theological Dictionary of the New Testament* Vol. 3. Grand Rapids, MI: Wm. B. Eerdmans Publishing, Co., 1966.

Brown, Robert E. *Edwards and the Bible.* Bloomington, IN: Indiana University Press, 2002.

Bruce, F.F *The Epistle to the Hebrews.* The New International Commentary on the New Testament. Grand Rapids, MI: Wm. B. Eerdmans Publishing, Co., 1964.

Brueggemann, Walter. *Genesis.* Interpretation. James L. Mayes, ed. Atlanta, GA: John Knox Press, 1982.

Carson, D.A. *Becoming Conversant With the Emerging Church.* Grand Rapids, MI: Zondervan Publishing, 2005.

Chalmers, Thomas. *The Works of Thomas Chalmers, Complete in One Volume.* A. Towar, Hogan and Thompson Publishing, 1833

Chamberlain, Ava D. "Self-Deception as a Theological Problem in Jonathan Edwards's 'Treatise Concerning Religious Affections.'" *Church History* 63 (4):541–56, 1994.

Cherry, Conrad C. *The Theology of Jonathan Edwards, A Reappraisal.* Forward by Stephen J. Stein and new introduction by Conrad C. Cherry, 1990. Bloomington and Indianapolis, IN: Indiana University Press, 1966.

Childs, Brevard S. *The Book of Exodus.* Louisville, KY: The Westminster Press, 1974.

Clydesdale, Tim. *The First Year Out.* Chicago: University of Chicago Press, 2007.

Delattre, Ronald A. *Beauty and Sensibility in the Thought of Jonathan Edwards.* New Haven, CT: Yale University Press. Reprint, Eugene, Oregon: Wipf & Stock, 1968.

Delitzsch, Franz. *Psalms.* Commentary on the Old Testament In Ten Volumes. Vol. 5. Grand Rapids, MI: Wm B. Eerdman's Publishing Company, 1867. Reprint 1988.

DeYoung, Kevin and Kluck, Ted. *Why We're Not Emergent.* Chicago: Moody Publishers, 2008.

Durham, John I. *Exodus.* Word Biblical Commentary. Dallas, TX: Word Books Publishers, 1987.

Edwards, Jonathan. *The Works of Jonathan Edwards,* Vol 2, *A Treatise Concerning Religious Affections.* Edited by John E. Smith. New Haven, CT: Yale University Press, 1959.

_____. *The Works of Jonathan Edwards,* Vol. 16, *Letters and Personal Writings.* Edited by George S. Claghorn. New Haven, CT: Yale University Press, 1998.

_____. *The Works of Jonathan Edwards.* Vol. 4, *Great Awakening.* Edited by C.C. Goen. New Haven, CT: Yale University Press, 1957.

_____. *The Works of Jonathan Edwards,* Vol. 6, *Scientific and Philosophical Writings.* Edited by Wallace E. Anderson. New Haven, CT: Yale University Press 1980.

Elwell, Walter A. *Baker Encyclopedia of the Bible,* Vol. 1. Grand Rapids, MI: Baker Book House, 1988.

Feagin, Susan L. "Aesthetics" in *The Cambridge Dictionary of Philosophy*. Cambridge: Cambridge University Press, 1995.

Fretheim, Terence E. *Exodus*. Interpretation. Louisville, KY: John Knox Press, 1991.

Hanger, Donald A. *Matthew 1–13*. Word Biblical Commentary. Dallas, TX: Word Books, 1993.

Hatch, Nathan O., Stout, Harry S., eds. *Jonathan Edwards and the American Experience*. Oxford: Oxford University Press, 1988

Hendriksen, William. *Matthew*. New Testament Commentary. Grand Rapids, MI: Baker Book House, 1973.

Hughes, Philip Edgcumbe. *Paul's Second Epistle to the Corinthians*. The New International Commentary on the New Testament. Grand Rapids, MI: Wm. B. Eerdmans Publishing, Co, 1962.

Kidner, Derek. *Genesis*. Tyndale Old Testament Commentaries. Downers Grove, IL: InterVarsity Press, 1967.

_____. *Psalms 1–72*. Tyndale Old Testament Commentaries. Downers Grove, IL: InterVarsity Press, 1973.

Kistemaker, Simon J. *Exposition of the Epistle to the Hebrews*. New Testament Commentary. Grand Rapids, MI: Baker Book House, 1984.

_____. *Peter and Jude*. New Testament Commentary. Grand Rapids, MI: Baker Book House, 1987.

Koester, Craig R. *Hebrews*. The Anchor Bible. New York: Doubleday, 2001.

Lane, William L. *Hebrews 9–13*. Word Biblical Commentary. Dallas, TX: Word Books, 1991.

Lee, Sang Hyung, Guelzo, Allen C., eds. *Edwards in Our Time: Jonathan Edwards and the Shaping of American Religion*. Grand Rapids, MI: Wm. B. Eerdmans Publishing, Co., 1999.

Marsden, George M. *Jonathan Edwards: A Life*. New Haven, CT: Yale University Press, 2003.

_____. *A Short Life of Jonathan Edwards*. Grand Rapids, MI.: Wm. B. Eerdmans Publishing, Co., 2008.

McLaren, Brian D. *A New Kind of Christianity*. New York: HarperCollins Publishing, 2010.

Miller, Perry. *Jonathan Edwards*. Lincoln, NE: University of Nebraska Press, 1949.

Mitchell, Louis J. "The Theological Aesthetics of Jonathan Edwards," *Theology Today* 64: 36–46, 2007.

Moody, Josh. *Jonathan Edwards and the Enlightenment*. Lanham, MD: University Press of America, 2005.

Morris, Leon. *The Gospel According to Matthew*. Grand Rapids, MI: Wm. B. Eerdmans Publishing, Co., 1992.

Motyer, Alec J. *Isaiah*. Tyndale Old Testament Commentaries. Downers Grove, IL: InterVarsity Press, 1999.

Mounce, Robert H. *The Book of Revelation*. The New International Commentary on the New Testament. Grand Rapids, MI: Wm. B. Eerdmans Publishing, Co., 1977.

Oswalt, John N. *The Book of Isaiah Chapters 1–39*. The New International Commentary on the Old Testament. Grand Rapids, MI: Wm. B. Eerdmans Publishing, Co., 1986.

Penner, Myron B. "Jonathan Edwards and Emotional Knowledge of God," *Direction* 30 (1): 63-75, 2001.

Robertson, O. Palmer. *The Books of Nahum, Habakkuk and Zephaniah*. The New International Commentary on the New Testament. Grand Rapids, MI: Wm. B. Eerdmans Publishing, Co., 1990.

Scaramanga, Url. "R.I.P Emerging Church." *Christianity Today Online*, September, 2008, https://www.christianitytoday.com/pastors/2008/september-online-only/rip-emerging-church.html

Seel, David John. *The New Copernicans*. Nashville, TN: Thomas Nelson, 2018.

Sire, James W. *The Universe Next Door*. Downers Grove, IL: InterVarsity Press, 1997.

Smith, Christian. *Soul Searching*. New York: Oxford University Press (Electronic Edition), 2005.

Smith, Ralph L. *Micah – Malachi*. Word Biblical Commentary. Waco, TX: Word Books, 1984.

Sweeney, Douglas A. *Edwards the Exegete*. New York, NY: Oxford University Press, 2016.

Taylor, Charles. *A Secular Age*. Cambridge, MA and London: The Belknap Press of Harvard University, 2007.

Tracy, Patricia J. *Jonathan Edwards, Pastor: Religion and Society in Eighteenth-Century Northampton*. Jonathan Edwards Classic Studies. New York: Hill and Wang, 1980.

VanGemeren, Willem. *The Progress of Redemption*. Grand Rapids, MI: Academe Books, 1988.

Watts, John D.W. *Isaiah 1–33*. Word Biblical Commentary. Waco, TX: Word Books, 1985.

Webber, Robert E. *The Younger Evangelicals*. Grand Rapids, MI: Baker Books, 2002.

Webber, Robert E., ed. *Listening to the Beliefs of Emerging Churches*. Grand Rapids, MI: Zondervan Publishing, 2007.

Weiser, Arthur. *The Psalms*. The Old Testament Library. Philadelphia, PA: WestminsterPress, 1962.

Index

Below is a brief index of significant persons, places, doctrines, titles and topics.

A Divine and Supernatural Light, 70, 206
adolescents, 200
aesthetics, 6, 152, 205
affections, 5, 41, 55, 57–59, 63, 66, 69, 70, 77, 79, 80, 86, 90, 100, 108, 142, 152, 155, 156, 203, 204
affective faith, 205
Alter, Robert, 29
Ames, William, 125
Anglicanism, 109
anti-intellectualism, 70
appetite, 84, 85
Arminianism, 109
art, 65
Aslan, 183
assurance of salvation, 63
Augustine of Hippo, 98
authentic faith, 3, 177, 178, 184
authenticity, 200

awakening, 108

Barth, Karl, 98
beauty, 69, 72, 73, 81, 96, 142, 155, 157, 170, 183, 194, 195, 198, 204
Bible, 141
biblical anthropology, 145
blasphemy against Holy Spirit, 38, 39
boredom, 204
Browne, Daniel, 114
Brueggerman, Walter, 15, 16
Burke, John, 135, 136

Calvin, John, 148, 151
Calvinism, 111, 116, 149, 203
Campolo, Tony, 196, 197
Carson, D. A., 3, 128, 129
Chalmers, Thomas, 74
Chauncy, Charles, 146, 147
Cherry, Conrad, 4, 69, 88, 125

Christian experience, 27
Christian practice, 87, 88, 93
church membership, 103, 107, 108, 114, 120
class divisions, 119
classical Christianity, 134
Clydesdale, Tim, 153–155
Coleman, Benjamin, 118
Connecticut Collegiate School, 107, 114
consent, 68, 99
conversion, 100
conviction, 71
covenant, 115
covenant, old and new, 45
curriculum, 156

Davenport, James, 146, 147
Delattre, Roland, 60, 61, 69, 98, 99
Descartes, Rene, 125, 127, 152
desire, 55, 85, 86, 100, 183
DeYoung, Kevin, 129
disenchantment, 139
dispositions, 41, 63, 108
Driscoll, Mark, 131, 136
Durham, John, 19

economic realities, 120
Edwards, Timothy, 103, 104
Edwards' preaching style, 113
Emergent Church, 3, 6, 114, 127, 128, 131, 132, 138–140, 149
emotionalism, 57, 60, 61, 70
empiricism, 110
enchantment, 142
Enlightenment, 117, 126, 134, 139, 143–145, 149

Essay Concerning Human Understanding, 114
evangelism, 170, 194
evil, 39
excellency, 156
experiential faith, 114
external religion, 172

faculties, 59
faith, 60, 66, 115, 195
Faithful Narrative, 106, 118
Franklin, Benjamin, 125, 148, 205
free choice, 60
Frudakis, Zenos, 185, 186, 189

gracious affections, 83, 87
Great Awakening, 86, 108, 110, 118, 204

habitual love, 41
half-way covenant, 105, 113, 127
harmony, 69
Haroutunian, Joseph, 148
Hatch, Nathan, 141
heart, 26, 38, 55, 183
Hendriksen, William, 39
hermeneutics, 136
holiness, 32, 51, 87, 100
Hughes, Philip, 44
humiliation, 73
Hunter, Todd, 128

idealism, 114
image of God, 48
inclination, 42, 59, 60, 69, 142, 152, 156, 203
individualism, 121, 122, 145, 148

Johnson, Samuel, 114

Index

joy, 94
judgment, 36

Keller, Tim, 21, 170
Kidner, Derek, 15, 16, 27, 28
Kimball, Brian, 138
Kimball, Dan, 131
Kistemaker, Simon, 50

land availability, 121
Lane, William, 42, 43
leadership, 124
Lewis, C. S., 182
Locke, John, 71, 109–111, 114, 116, 125

magic, 116
marriage, 123
Marsden, George, 58, 121
materialism, 115
McLaren, Brian, 127, 129, 131, 137, 148
means of grace, 90, 92
mechanistic worldview, 115
Millennials, 139
Miller, Perry, 70, 71, 96, 109, 111, 113, 115
Mitchell, Louis, 68
Modernism, 130, 143, 148
Moody, Josh, 143–145
moral excellency, 52, 68
moral holiness, 20
moral perfections, 99
motivation, 42
Motyer, Alec, 35
mystery, 129
mysticism, 60, 70, 86

Narnia, 182

National Survey of Youth and Religion, 200, 202
Native Americans, 120
natural affections, 77, 83
natural excellency, 68
natural perfections, 99
natural sciences, 205
natural sense, 64
natural sight, 171
naturalism, 114, 205
New Copernicans, 127, 139, 142–144, 149, 204
New Lights, 57, 96
new sense, 63, 94, 108, 142
Newton, Isaac, 109, 114–116, 125
Nietzsche, Friedrich, 143
Northampton, 79, 104, 110, 118, 120–122, 153
nova effect, 138, 140

objectivity, 114
Old Lights, 58, 96, 125, 146
orthodoxy, 60

Pagitt, Doug, 131, 132
passions, 205
Penner, Myron, 203
perception, 59, 60, 64, 69
Personal Narrative, 91, 107
Pharisees, 39
political revolution, 124
Postmodernism, 6, 114, 125, 126, 130, 143, 145, 148, 205
practical theology, 112
Pragmatic Evangelicals, 134
pragmatism, 2
prayer, 62, 183
pre-critical faith, 133

Pre-modern, 125, 133
presence as beauty, 27
primary beauty, 69, 99
propositionalism, 134, 136
public worship, 169

regeneration, 60
relativism, 133
relevant worship services, 202
Religious Affections, 10, 28, 49, 52, 57–59, 89, 91, 92, 100, 108, 143, 145, 157, 206
religious experience, 34, 78
religious revolution, 124
repentance, 64
restoration, 48
revival, 58, 70, 106, 118
reward, 42, 43

sacraments, 62
sacrifice, 170
science, 116
search for authenticity, 135
secondary beauty, 69, 99
Seel, David, 127, 139
self-interest, 66, 88
sensation, 58
sermons, 96
Shema, 41
Shepard, Thomas, 125
Sibbes, Richard, 125
Sinners in the Hands of an Angry God, 97, 112, 114
Smith, Christian, 200, 201
Smith, John E., 58, 88, 89, 155
soul, 29
speculative knowledge, 112
speculative religion, 112

speculative theology, 101
spiritual discernment, 71
spiritual discoveries, 16
spiritual health, 180
spiritual joy, 51
spiritual pride, 75, 76
spiritual sense, 30, 63, 179
spiritual sight, 171
Stein, Stephen, 4, 124
Stoddard, Colonel John, 105
Stoddard, Solomon, 104, 118, 119
subjectivism, 148
Sweeney, Douglas, 141
symmetry, 81, 83

Taylor, Charles, 138, 140
technologia, 109
The Distinguishing Marks of a Work of the Spirit of God, 147
The Mind, 68, 110
Thomas Aquinas, 98
tongue, 38
Tracy, Patricia, 121–123
Traditional Evangelicals, 134
trials, 93
true religion, 27

Vineyard USA, 128
Voyage of the Dawn Treader, 182

Ward, Karen, 136
Webber, Robert, 2, 132–135, 148
Whitefield, George, 146
Williams, Elisha, 109
works of the Spirit, 57
worldview, 6

Yale, 109, 110, 117, 141

Yale library, 109
Younger Evangelicals, 6, 117, 132, 134, 139, 200

youth, 153

www.ingramcontent.com/pod-product-compliance
Lightning Source LLC
Chambersburg PA
CBHW071353290426
44108CB00014B/1530